GW00644810

ISBN 978-9974-91-853-5

We are Juan Ignacio Pita and Claire O'Brien, and we have spent most of our adult lives travelling around the world, living in different countries.

Including Uruguay we have the combined experience of having lived in 7 different countries, each containing its own unique set of challenges, but our move to Uruguay was different for both of us. As Juan is a native Montevidean, we had the rare perspective of an expat combined with a local point of view.

Of course there were bumps on the road. Returning to his homeland, Juan faced mixed emotions, as he needed to strike a balance between his old customs and his new ones. On the other hand, for Claire, coming to a new country with someone who already knew the setup, meant going through the usual steps of moving country, but without a lot of the excitement of discovery.

In the end this combination of experience worked well for us, and we relished all of our victories big and small, from completing the visa process, to making our first *asado* together. We were left with the thrilling sensation of having found **new ways to do the same things**.

MILESTONES

HOW TO USE THIS GUIDE

This book is written from the perspective of a local and an expat, which gives a unique insight into the entire process of moving to Uruguay. Claire's status as an expat meant that we needed to go through all of the usual official procedures needed when moving country and Juan's local know-how provided a cultural insight that is indispensable when learning how to function in Uruguayan society.

As a huge part of the process of moving abroad is discovery, we wanted to provide a taste of what you can expect and of what you will need in Uruguay, in an easy-to-read manner. To do this we have combined descriptions with links to websites and mobile apps, so that you can easily find the information that is important to you when you need it. For some of these links, we have used short links, which will appear in this format: **goo.gl**. These will connect you to a very specific part of a website. Websites in English (EN) or any other language are also few and far between, so you should **assume that all links are in Spanish**, unless we have indicated otherwise.

As the language barrier will be a huge issue for many people, we have also included relevant words in Uruguayan Spanish, to give you a hand in communicating what you really want.

While reading this guide you will notice that prices are written in Uruguayan Pesos ($) and US Dollars (USD), as the use of USD along with the local currency gives readers a better idea of how much things cost.

The rate used is:
USD 1 to $ 30

Keep in mind that the rate of USD has been fluctuating within a margin of 5% over the last year, so it's a good idea to check the current rate to give yourself a more accurate idea of prices.

If you have any comments, thoughts or suggestions about this book we would be delighted to hear from you. Send us an email at **info.feelingabroad@gmail.com**.

We have put a lot of time and effort into this book. Please help us to continue this work by not giving it away for free.

THE BASICS

The *República Oriental del Uruguay* (Eastern Republic o Uruguay) is a small country nestled between Brazil an Argentina. It is made up of 19 departments, all of whic contribute a different flavour to the country. The south is largel dominated by Montevideo, the capital city, which is where th majority of the population lives.

A Brief History

Uruguayan history is not a complex one. Having been fought ove in a series of small battles by the Spanish and Portuguese, it we finally declared independent in 1828. During this time th country went from strength to strength, becoming one of th most liberal countries in the region. Some high points on the list of achievements include the educational reform in 1877 whe primary education became compulsory, and the separation state from Church in 1919.

Prior to European settlement Uruguay was home to sever different indigenous tribes. The Guaraní and Charrúa are th main groups that Uruguayans identify with today, though only 2.4% of the population can legitimately claim descent. As the native tribes proved to be too much of an inconvenience to the European settlers, most of the population was eradicated in 1833.

Uruguay's more recent history has been marked by a military dictatorship which lasted from 1973 to 1985. Though it ended 30 years ago this period is still fresh in the minds of many.

Since the dictatorship Uruguay has returned to being a fully functioning democracy and has recently claimed a place on the world stage with controversial laws such as the legalisation of marijuana.

Public Holidays

The link below contains a list of Uruguayan public holidays. Keep in mind that January 1st, May 1st, July 18th, August 25th and December 25th are the only guaranteed days off. All other days are given at the discretion of your employer.

goo.gl/I9hUZT

Uruguayan Country Codes

Uruguay's internet domain is *.uy.*

The international calling code is +598.

25 Things you should know about Uruguay:

1 Uruguay means "River of the Painted Birds".

2 The population of Uruguay is approximately 3.5 million.

3 Montevideo is the capital of Uruguay, and although it only spans 0.3% of the total area of the land, it is home to 40% of the country's population.

4 Uruguay is home to 77,000 non-nationals (according to the 2011 census). 47,000 of these come from other South American countries, 18,200 from Spain and Italy and 2,800 from the USA.

10 Traditional dances include the *"Pericón"* and the *"Gato"*.

11 *"Truco"* is the name of the national card game, and is played using Spanish cards, not poker ones.

12 Famous Uruguayans include José Mujica, Mario Benedetti, Carlos Gardel, Alcides Ghiggia, Luis Suárez, Diego Forlán, Jorge Drexler, Eduardo Galeano, Natalia Oreiro, Enzo Francescoli, Carlos Páez Vilaró, Fernando Parrado, Álvaro Recoba, Héctor Scarone, Juan Alberto Schiaffino, Joaquín Torres García, Alfredo Zitarrosa and China Zorrilla.

5 The median age of the total population is about 34 years old.

6 There are more than 500 centenarians living in Uruguay.

7 Uruguayans were the creators of the Lap of Honor (*Vuelta Olímpica*) in 1924, futsal in 1930 and a portable heating element called *SUN* in 1962.

8 The Tango and the Milonga originated between the borders of Uruguay and Argentina at the end of the 19th century.

9 The famous tango *"La Cumparsita"* was written by a Uruguayan musician in 1916.

13 The 16 survivors of the Andes plane crash in 1972 were Uruguayan.

14 Uruguay was the world's first nation to legalize the production, sale, and consumption of cannabis.

15 Uruguay and Argentina share the widest river in the world, the *Río de la Plata*.

16 The Uruguayan national football team has the most titles in the world with 2 World Cups, 2 Olympic Games and 15 Copa Americas. It also hosted the first ever Fifa World Cup.

17 Uruguay exported over 16 million cans of corned beef in 1943, making this product world famous in the 20th century.

18 Uruguay has the longest carnival in the world, lasting over 40 days.

19 The consumption of meat is 99 kilos per person per year.

20 Uruguay is the top country in the world for the number of cattle per person, coming in at around 4 cattle per capita.

21 Uruguayans are the main consumers of *yerba mate*, with a consumption of 10 kilos per year/person, though Uruguay doesn't actually grow any yerba of its own.

22 Uruguayans are the 2nd biggest consumers of whisky per capita.

23 Catedral hill is the highest point in Uruguay, reaching 514 meters.

24 Uruguay is the fifth highest consumer of fizzy drinks with 113 litres per capita/year.

25 Uruguay ranks 8th on the world list for the most guns owned per capita (according to statistics from 2014), with 32 guns for every 100 people.

QUALITY OF LIFE

For many who have never lived there, Uruguay is viewed as a retiree's paradise: full of beaches, bold political choices and virgin land as far as the eye can see. However the reality is quite different. As with every country on earth, Uruguay has its pros and cons and before you go, it is a good idea to decide on your priorities and see if the balance is right for you. For example although the pollution and unemployment are low, the crime rate is relatively high.

Your quality of life will also be impacted by whether you choose to live in the countryside or in a city, as the ease of access in Montevideo is drastically different from in the country, though the crime rate in the countryside is much lower than that of the capital.

To help put all of this into perspective we have compiled some statistics on how Uruguay compares on the world stage in terms of quality of life. The charts are based on world averages and are designed to provide a context on how they can affect your quality of life.

Life Expectancy - **77 years** - *Great*

Air Pollution - **40 (index)** - *Good*

Unemployment - **7.7%** - *Good*

Inflation Rate - **6.55%** - *Moderate*

Purchasing Power - **45 (index)** - *Moderate*

Safety - **44 (index)** - *Moderate*

Commute Time - **45 mins** - *Moderate*

CHOOSING A FLIGHT

Booking a flight will be one of your first big milestones in moving. Reserving a long distance, largely non-refundable plane ticket normally brings everything into focus and makes the whole experience feel more real. It will give you a definite time frame to organise yourself in and a better idea of your budget.

Choosing the correct flight and airline can mean the difference between starting your adventure laughing or crying.

Traveling 10 or more hours in a confined space with little sleep while being in a delicate emotional state from saying goodbye to your loved ones, and having to fight tooth and nail with the air staff because you want a glass of water is not the best way to start a new life.

To that end we would recommend the following websites to find the best combinations of quality, price and time for your flight. Remember to find the best price, always cross reference with the airline's website.

www.skyscanner.net   www.momondo.com

While searching for your flight, try to balance the price with the journey time. Adding 5 hours to your flight for the sake of saving USD 50 might seem like a good idea now, but you will probably regret it while you are sitting in an airport for those 5 extra hours.

Other factors to take into consideration are the weight allowances for each company for both your hand luggage and your check-in luggage. Every bit of extra weight allowance is invaluable when planning a move abroad.

If you have a connecting flight make sure to check the luggage policy of each company as some companies don't have luggage agreements. You don't want to find you are 5 kilos overweight with one of the companies when it's too late.

On the following websites you can look at customer reviews fo
different airlines. These reviews will tell you everything fro
the punctuality of the airline to the quality of the food serve
on board.

www.airlinequality.com   www.worldairlineawards.com

Choosing the correct seat can also be a major concern for som
travellers, particularly if you are a nervous flier or if you like
stretch out on planes. The following websites give detailed ma
of each kind of plane so that you can assess the comfort leve
of different flights you might be looking into.

www.seatguru.com   www.seatexpert.com

INTERNATIONAL SHIPPING

Before moving to Uruguay it is important to decide what to do with the belongings you can't fit into your suitcase: Do you ship them or throw them out?

When making this decision it is important to take into consideration that most apartments and houses in Uruguay will come completely unfurnished. The cost of furnishing your home from scratch is also massive, as commodity prices are quite high. For this reason we would recommend shopping around for a good international moving company and coming with at least the bare essentials of furniture.

If you decide to ship, getting your possessions to Uruguay is very complicated, so it's a good idea to give yourself plenty of time to get things organised.

Moving Companies

There are many dedicated overseas moving companies to make shipping your belongings easier. For quotes and comparisons on international moving companies check the websites below.

www.intlmovers.com

www.reallymoving.com

www.internationalmoving.com

Remember that your belongings can take as long as six weeks to arrive so you need to plan well in advance. Before you ship, please be aware that your goods must arrive either within 6 months of your arrival, or no more than 3 months before. Goods should also have been shipped from the same country of origin as the owner and will not be released from customs until the owner has arrived in Uruguay.

Required Documents

One of the biggest snags you'll hit while shipping to Uruguay are the complicated customs regulations.

Before you ship you need to make sure you have the following documents, or there will be problems once your belongings reach Uruguay. These documents must be submitted to the Customs Authority either by the owner of the goods, or an authorised representative.

You will need:

➡ An itemised inventory in Spanish, which has been legalised by the Uruguayan Consulate in the country of origin.

➡ A bank guarantee letter to the value of the potential tax you will need to pay on the goods you are shipping. This will be returned to you after you have obtained residence status. We will cover which goods are taxable further on in this section.

To get started you will first need to find a Customs agent (*Despachante de Aduana*) in Uruguay. These are professionals in handling the ins and outs of Uruguayan customs. For more information on finding an agent, check the following link:

www.adau.com.uy

For more information on Customs procedures you can contact the authorities at info@aduanas.gub.uy or check the Customs website: goo.gl/GaJEli

CUSTOMS OFFICES IN URUGUAY

Montevideo Customs Office
Rambla 25 de Agosto, No 199
Accessible via Yacaré street.
Open from 9.00 – 17.00.

If you are outside Montevideo, you can check this link for the Customs Directory: **goo.gl/PThrE7**

Dutiable/ Restricted Items

Electrical Appliances

New electrical appliances are prohibited and used electrical appliances are restricted items, with only one of each item being allowed. There is however an exception for TV sets, where you may bring more than one.

Sporting Guns

Sporting guns are allowed so long as you have acquired a permit from the Ministry of Defence. All other weapons are prohibited.

Wedding Gifts

Wedding gifts require a separate packing list and a notarized marriage certificate.

Household Goods

New household goods are subject to duties and value added tax, but used items are duty free.
Please also keep in mind that if you wish to ship bicycles, they will be allowed as a part of a shipment of household goods.

Inherited Goods

Inherited goods also require a separate packing list, along with a notarized proof of estate and death certificate.

Other Items

Items such as works of art, antiques, jewellery and coins are restricted to what the Custom's authorities deem to be a reasonable amount. Any more than that will be subject to duty.

Alcohol and tobacco products are subject to duty. All food must have the appropriate clearance certificates issued by Uruguayan Custom's Authorities.

PROHIBITED ITEMS

The following items are prohibited by Customs in Uruguay:

- ⇒ New electrical appliances
- ⇒ Drugs
- ⇒ Pornographic or subversive materials
- ⇒ Plants (without the appropriate health certificates)

MOTOR VEHICLES

There are strict regulations surrounding the importation of moto vehicles.

All new cars are dutiable. To import them you need:

- ⇒ the original purchase invoice
- ⇒ the Certificate of Title and Registration

All of these documents must be legalised by the Uruguaya Consulate at origin, as well as being officially translated int Spanish. These translations must be provided by an offici translator registered in Uruguay.

Non Uruguayan citizens are not permitted to import use vehicles, unless you meet one of the following criteria:

- ⇒ You are a retiree with a monthly income of at least US 1,500, obtained from abroad.
- ⇒ You own a property in Uruguay to the value of US 100,000 (purchased after the enactment law 16.340).
- ⇒ You have bought USD 100,000 worth of government stoc from Uruguay.

Remember that you can only import one car, and that you a not permitted to sell it for 10 years after importation.

NOTE - Customs regulations are subject to change at any time.

RESTRICTED ITEMS

Uruguay is quite strict about the items you can bring in with you and though you will not have any problems with personal items, bringing things such as gifts may cause problems if they are above a certain value. Before you pack, read the guidelines below to find out what you can and cannot carry.

Restricted Items

The following items are restricted in Uruguay. You may not carry them with you unless you have gone through the official importation process:

- Plants, plant parts or any related products.
- Fresh fruit and vegetables.
- Seeds, or items made using seeds
- Flowers, ornamental plants and in vitro cultures.
- Earth, fruit trees, fodder, branches, stakes, spikes, bulbs, buds or any other organic material.
- Animals and animal products or by-products (butter, eggs, cream, cheese, etc).
- Liquid milk (except for long life milk)
- Animal feed and biological or veterinary products.
- Flammables, alkaloids, narcotics, obscene objects, and subversive or pornographic materials.
- Pets: birds, exotic specimens, bees, etc (cats and dogs are not included in this).
- Property that does not belong to the passenger.

Items to Declare

Travellers coming into Uruguay from abroad do not have to declare items such as clothes, personal items, books and brochures, unless they're for commercial use.

For all other items, travellers coming from Argentina, Brazil, Chile and Paraguay have a tax free allowance of USD 300, while all other countries enjoy an allowance of USD 500. For passengers under 18, only 50% of this allowance is applicable. Remember that this allowance is only available once a year.

If you are travelling with a lot of extra items, it is always a good idea to bring receipts to clear up any potential misunderstandings with Customs.

Please note that there is also an additional allowance of USD 300 on products bought in duty free shops, with limitations on products such as cigarettes and alcoholic beverages from outside the Mercosur area. For these products there is an allowance of 2 cartons of cigarettes and 2 litres of alcohol per person.

Mobile Phones

You need to declare your mobile phone at Customs if you are going to use a Uruguayan sim card.

Declaring your Items

If you have anything to declare, check for the sign saying "*Aduanas*" after you have picked up your luggage.

If you have any further questions or concerns about Customs you can contact the Customer Care Centre at **info@aduanas.gub.uy**. Make sure to contact them with plenty of time so you have your answer before your flight.

CONVERTING YOUR CURRENCY

The currency of Uruguay is the Uruguayan Peso ($). Peso coins come in denominations of $1, $2, $5, $10 and $50. Pesos also come in notes of $20, $50, $100, $200, $500, $1,000 and $2,000.

Before you arrive in Uruguay, getting your hands on pesos may prove a difficult task, as it is not a popular currency outside of Uruguay. Uruguayan Pesos can be requested through your bank, though many will not guarantee that they can get them for you. To save yourself hassle, we recommend arriving with Euro or USD and exchanging them once you arrive.

Currencies from nearby countries such as Argentinian Peso and Brazilian Real are also widely accepted by exchange offices. Keep in mind that USD is accepted in most major shops and restaurants, so it's probably the best currency to have before you can get some pesos.

You can get an idea of current rates from the Bank of Uruguay linked below.

www.brou.com.uy

At the Airport

In most airports in the world, exchange rates are less favourable than in the city, but fortunately in Carrasco Airport there are two options for converting your currency:

The first option is a place called **Global Exchange**. There are 2 of these, one located just beyond the luggage collection hall and the other just past Customs. The rates here are normally less favourable than city ones.

The option we recommend is a place called **Abitab**. This is a convenience store located in the Arrivals Hall, where you can exchange your currency at the same rates you will find in the city centre.

It's important however to note that Abitab is not a 24 hour shop. Its opening hours are **Mondays** to **Saturdays** between **8.00** and **20.00** and **Sundays** between **8.00** and **16.00**. If the Abitab is already closed when you arrive, we recommend going to Global Exchange and exchanging the minimum amount necessary for your trip to your accommodation and getting the rest later on.

Once in the city, make sure to shop around a bit first before exchanging your money. It's not recommended to exchange money in the banks as their rates are fixed. Currency exchange offices on the other hand often fix rates to be more in your favour to try and inspire customer loyalty. This of course requires a little bit of haggling. Don't worry though, it is common practice and can be done after you have been given a price by simply asking: *"¿Me lo podés mejorar?"* (Can you give me a better rate?)

Alternatively you can open negotiations straight away by asking: *"¿Qué es lo mejor que me podés hacer por cambiar XXX pesos?"* (What is the best rate you can give me for changing XX to pesos?)

In Uruguay authorized money exchanges will never charge commission and the exchange rates will be posted on big screens inside the shop, most of which will be visible from the street.

The Seasons

Uruguay has a warm, humid climate with 4 distinct seasons.

SUMMER (22th December to 21th March)

Summer is normally very hot and sticky. Temperatures usually range between 16°C (61°F) and 32°C (90°F). A lot of the time it will feel much hotter because of the humidity, with the region north of the Río Negro experiencing the highest temperatures. During this period locals and tourists alike will generally visit the towns and cities dotted along the 650 km of coastline.

Although temperatures will never be too severe, you do need to look out for the UV rays. They are extremely high in Uruguay and the sun can be very dangerous. It's advised to avoid direct exposure to the sun between the hours of 11.00 to 17.00.

In summer there is an average of 13.5 hours of daylight every day with around 10 hours of sunlight.

AUTUMN (22th March to 21th June)

Autumn is one of the most pleasant times of year with the temperatures dropping to a max of 21°C (70°F) and a minimum of 8°C (46°F). At night the cold makes the air feel fresher, though every week the days will grow shorter.

In autumn there is an average of 11 hours of daylight and 6.5 hours of sunlight every day.

WINTER (22th June to 21th September)

Winter is mostly cold and humid. Temperatures normally stay between 14°C (57°F) and 5°C (41°F) during the afternoon, though the real feel can occasionally plunge to as low as -2°C (28°F). Between the months of July and October it is often windy, which can make the temperature feel much lower than it actually is. A coat, a woollen hat, a scarf and gloves are recommended to stay warm outside.

In winter there is a daily average of 10.5 hours of daylight and 6 hours of sunlight.

SPRING (22th September to 21th December

Spring is considered the best season, a temperatures begin to rise, though it is stil necessary to leave the house in a ligh jacket. It will normally stay between 10° (50°F) and 21°C (70°F).

During this time of the year there is a average of 13.5 hours of daylight and hours of sunlight on a daily basis.

Weather

We recommend moving to Uruguay during spring or autumn the weather is the easiest to get used to. To find out mor detailed information about the weather and climate, check the Uruguayan Meteorological Institute (*Instituto Uruguayo Meteorología*) website linked below.

www.inumet.gub.uy

To find out the weather on a day to day basis we recommer listening to the weather report on the news.

Warnings

The effects of sun in the southern hemisphere are very different from those in the northern hemisphere. **In Uruguay, the sun is very dangerous in the summer**, even during cloudy days. As a result it is recommended to avoid being exposed to the sun between the hours of 11.00 and 17.00, even if you are used to being in a sunny climate. If you are outside during these hours make sure to use a sun cream with high protection for both UVA and UVB rays, and keep as much skin covered as possible.

For more information check the Ministry of Public Health website.

goo.gl/TXTNFL

When visiting a **beach** remember to check the flag beside the lifeguard's cabin to see the water conditions for the day. The flag will either be red, yellow or green. A red flag means that the water is dangerous, so getting into the water is prohibited. A yellow means that the water is relatively safe, but all activities should be done with caution. It is a good idea to stay near the coast on these days. The green flag means that the water is safe, so you can proceed as normal.

As well as looking out for the sun, you will also need to keep an eye out for signs of electrical storms. These occur throughout the entire year, but are especially prevalent in August. Storms are usually accompanied by very heavy rain, strong winds and sometimes even hail. During these times don't be surprised to see people walking around with plastic bags tied to their feet.

Time

Uruguay's time zone is UTC -3.
As of October 2015, there is no daylight savings in Uruguay.

To find your own time zone, or any other in the world, check the website below.

www.24timezones.com

To live and work in Uruguay you must have a residence permit. Though the process itself is not complicated, if you don't speak Spanish things will get tricky. We recommend going through the process with someone who can interpret for you to make it as stress free as possible.

To apply for a permit you must go to the **Dirección Nacional de Migración**. In the following link you will find the locations of all migration offices in Uruguay and the requirements for all kinds of residence permits. Keep in mind that to get an appointment at the office in Montevideo, you may have to wait up to 2 months.

goo.gl/sDhSud

Obtaining a Residence Permit

There are many different options for getting a residence permit in Uruguay. These include visas for working, studying, rejoining family or for religious purposes. Once you have begun the process you will be issued with a certificate, with which you can apply for a temporary ID card (*Cédula de Identidad*). This will give you the same rights as a resident. Once the process is complete your temporary card will be replaced with a permanent one.

REQUIRED DOCUMENTS
Every kind of visa requires the following documents:

- Passport.
- Passport photo.
- Certificate of Health issued in Uruguay.
- Birth certificate.
- Police certificate.
- Proof of income.

Your birth cert and the police cert must be legalised. You must do this in your home country. Don't forget or else getting your residence in Uruguay will become a whole lot more difficult.

Documents for most nationalities, are legalised using an **apostille stamp**. However this option is not applicable for every nationality. For a full list of eligible countries check the link below.

goo.gl/E8avAZ

If your country is not in the apostille agreement, you must first get the document legalised in your country's Ministry of Foreign Affairs, and then in the Uruguayan Consulate closest to your home country. Once you reach Uruguay you must complete the process by getting the documents legalised in the Uruguayan Ministry of Foreign Affairs.

Any documents not in Spanish will also need to be translated. This must be done by a public translator in Uruguay. For more information on this have a look at our Suitable Translators section.

Additional documents may also be required depending on what kind of visa you are applying for. We'll give an outline of the individual permits, though for full details you should check the **Migration** website:

goo.gl/gfRzHt

Application Fees

The cost of applying for residence will be marked in a unit called *Unidades Indexadas* (UI). This is a unit, used to measure fees and rates, whose value changes on a monthly basis. This means that the real cost of your application can change from month to month. To find the value of UI every month, check the Mortgage Bank of Uruguay website: **www.bhu.gub.uy**

The residence application fee for each kind of visa is 557.3 UI and the fee for the certificate to apply for the Uruguayan ID (*Cédula de Identidad*) is 55.7 UI.

The residence process can take up to one year. If you want to leave the country in this time you must request a reentry permit. The fee for this is 345 UI.

Temporary Residence Permit (*Residencia Legal Temporaria*)

This visa covers anyone coming to Uruguay for the purpose of work, study, research or religion. To find out which additional documents you need skip down to the category which suits you.

Employees

This is for anyone who wants to find a job in Uruguay, including artists, journalists and professional sports people. It also includes people transferring directly into a Uruguayan company.

The additional documents you will need are as follows:

- ➡ Certificate of Health (*Carné de Salud*) issued by the Ministry of Public Health in Uruguay. These can be obtained at any official clinic.
- ➡ Proof of employment with the company. This should also contain details of your income and the duration of the contract. It must be signed by an authorized person in the company and contain the company letterhead.
- ➡ A notarized certificate with the legal details of the company.

Students

If you want to enter into full time studies in Uruguay you must also submit the following documents in addition to the aforementioned ones:

- ➡ Certificate of Health (*Carné de Salud*) issued by the Ministry of Public Health in Uruguay. These can be obtained at any official clinic.
- ➡ Official certificate of attendance from the school. If the institute is privately owned, you will also need to ask for a notarized certificate with the legal details of the institute.
- ➡ Proof that you can support yourself financially.

Researchers and Specialised Fields

Specialised professions include scientists, doctors, technicians, researchers, teachers or any other profession with a specialised knowledge employed either publically or privately.

The additional documents you will need are as follows:

- ➡ Certificate of Health (*Carné de Salud*) issued by the Ministry of Public Health in Uruguay. These can be obtained at any official health clinic.
- ➡ The details of your research/development in the country. This should also include details of your salary and the duration of your work. This must be presented on an official letter (complete with a letterhead) from the company you work for and signed by the authorized person.
- ➡ A notarized certificate with the legal details of the company will also be required if the company is a private one.

Missionaries

Anyone in Uruguay for religious purposes must submit the following additional documents:

➡ Certificate of Health (*Carné de Salud*) issued by the Ministry of Public Health in Uruguay. These can be obtained at any official clinic.

➡ Certificate issued by the Church stating your proposed activities and how long you intend on staying. This should be notarized and also include the legal details of the Church. The certificate should also contain the Church's official letterhead.

Permanent Residence Permit
(*Residencia Legal Permanente*)

A permanent residence permit can be issued to anyone who can demonstrate their intention of staying long term in Uruguay, be it because of family connections, or just because you like the place. This can be done by showing you have the financial means to support yourself. If you have children under 18, you must also show that they are in school.

Permits obtained because of familial links are divided into two categories: naturalised Uruguayans and Uruguayan nationals.

To find out what kind of additional documents you need check the category which applies to you below. Remember that all non Uruguayan documents need to be legalised, and also need to be translated by a public translator in Uruguay.

Spouse of a naturalised Uruguayan

- Marriage certificate.

Spouse of a Uruguayan National

- Marriage certificate.
- Birth cert of your spouse (the Uruguayan).
- Birth cert of the father or mother of your spouse (also on the Uruguayan side).

Legal Partner of a naturalised Uruguayan

- Certificate of partnership issued by a Uruguayan court.

Legal Partner of a Uruguayan National

- Certificate of partnership issued by a Uruguayan court.
- Birth cert of your partner (the Uruguayan).
- Birth cert of the father or mother of your partner (also on the Uruguayan side).

Widower/Widow a naturalised Uruguayan

- Death certificate of your spouse.
- Marriage Certificate.

Widower/Widow of a Uruguayan National

- Death certificate of your spouse.
- Marriage Certificate.
- Birth certificate of your spouse.
- Birth certificate of your spouse's parents.

Parents of a naturalised Uruguayan

- Birth cert of your child (naturalised Uruguayan).

Parents of a Uruguayan National

- Birth cert of the applicant's child (Uruguayan national).
- Birth cert of the parent of the child with Uruguayan nationality.

Grandchild of a naturalised Uruguayan

- Birth cert.
- Birth cert of your mother/father.
- Birth cert of your Uruguayan grandparent.

Grandchild of Uruguayan National

- Birth cert.
- Birth cert of your mother/father.
- Birth cert of your Uruguayan grandparent.
- Birth cert of your Uruguayan great grandparent.

Fee-Free Residence Permits

There is also an option for people with a Uruguayan relative to get a permanent residence permit for free (excluding translation and legalisation costs). This can be found on the website of the Ministry of Foreign Affairs, and applies to anyone with a close familial relationship with a Uruguayan (i.e. a child, spouse, parent or legal partner). This option also applies to citizens of Mercosur countries, regardless of their relationship to Uruguay.

This can be obtained by booking an appointment at either the **Ministry of Foreign Affairs located in Cuareim 1384 Montevideo**, or at the Consulate/Embassy in your country o origin. Each member of your family must be processed individually, but you should make all of the appointments fo the same day.

You will need to present documents such as birth certs or you marriage cert to prove the familial tie. Remember that if thes were not issued in Uruguay they should be legalised in your hom country and translated by a public translator in Uruguay.

For more information check the website of the Ministry of Foreig Affairs: **goo.gl/QAZUsY**. You can also contact the Ministry usin this email address: **consultaresidencias@mrree.gub.uy**.

Temporary Residence Permit (Mercosur)

Mercosur visas are available to citizens of Argentina, Brazi Chile, Bolivia, Ecuador, Colombia, Venezuela, Suriname an Guyana. To apply you will need all of the documents mentione above in the required documents section (except for the proof c income) in addition to the following documents and informatio

➡ Date of exact entry into Uruguay.

➡ Marriage certificate (if applicable).

➡ Certificate of naturalization (if applicable).

➡ Notarised permission to stay in Uruguay from your paren (if under 18 years of age).

Please note that this visa will only be issued for two years and must be renewed up to 90 days before it's due to expire. All documents should be presented as both an original and a copy and the ID you use should be the same one as you entered the country with.

Visa Free Passports

To know if you can stay in Uruguay without a visa, check the link below. This applies mostly to diplomatic and service passports.

goo.gl/lkuVhw

Citizens Information

For further questions contact: **atencionciudadana@agesic.gub.uy**

SUITABLE TRANSLATORS

In Uruguay all official documents are accepted in Spanish only unless they were issued in Brazil. If your documents are in any other language you will need to have them translated by a registered translator. This is a requirement of every institution in Uruguay. The documents should also be stamped by the translator in order to prove that they are official.

Translators must either be a member of the *Colegio de Traductores,* or a Uruguayan Consulate. You will normally find more than one translator per language so it is a good idea to ask for a few quotes to compare prices.

For a full list of translators check the following link:

www.colegiotraductores.org.uy

For a full list of Uruguayan Consulates see the link below:

goo.gl/iHjzSK

FINDING A JOB

Finding a job in Uruguay is very difficult if you don't speak Spanish, as the number of English speaking work environments is very limited. To that end, we would highly recommend going with a good level of Spanish to maximise your chances of finding something.

If you are lucky enough to find a job, **the normal working hours will be from 9.00 – 18.00**. In many jobs it is required to work a few hours on Saturdays, so take this into account when you are searching.

Below we have provided links to some of the most popular websites where you can find work in Uruguay. Before you arrive we recommend searching through job advertisements to make sure there are opportunities to match your skill set. However as **many companies prefer to interview face to face**, rather than by Skype, we would recommend holding off on applying for any jobs until you actually arrive. This way you can also update your CV with your Uruguayan address and phone number.

ull Time Work

Here we have provided links o websites offering full time obs. Most are posted in panish, though there are ome English ones.

www.buscojobs.com.uy
www.zonamerica.com EN/PT
www.aguadapark.com EN/PT
trabajo.gallito.com.uy
www.trabajando.com.uy
uy.indeed.com
www.opcionempleo.com.uy
www.uy.computrabajo.com

Recruitment Companies

For best results while job hunting, we recommend joining a recruitment company. This is particularly relevant for those who don't speak too much Spanish, as they will be able to save you from trawling through advertisements that you do not understand. Many recruitment companies will also do pre-interviews to prepare you for your interview with the actual firm.

www.advice.com.uy EN
www.adecco.com.uy
www.entrust.com.uy
ejobs.manpower.com.uy
capitalhumano.deloitte.com.

Starting your own Company

As in most countries, setting up a new business is a little bi tricky. If you do want to strike out on your own, you can ge everything registered at the following addresses:

BPS - www.bps.gub.uy
Registro de Contribuyentes y Empresas
Sarandí 570, Montevideo.

DGI - www.dgi.gub.uy
RUT Sector (located in the basemer
Fernández Crespo 1543, Montevideo

In order to register you first need to have your national ID (*Cédula de Identidad*). Make sure to register at least 10 days before you intend to commence business.

ZONAMERICA

Investing in Uruguay

If you are interested in investing in Uruguay, you can get all of the information you need off the website linked below. It is aimed at foreign investors, so it is also available in English and Portuguese.

www.uruguayxxi.gub.uy/invest EN/PT

Internships/Volunteer Opportunities

Internships and volunteer programs are a good way to get experience in your chosen field in an international environment. Though not so common in Uruguay, there are a few good opportunities.

goo.gl/AuKbcR   goo.gl/uFynBG

goo.gl/agHudM   goo.gl/BuOZc5

goo.gl/lD6bAQ

Next Steps

Once you have gotten an interview with a company the next step is setting your salary expectations. To get a good idea check around on job websites to see what other companies are offering for the same position.

For a quick frame of reference **the average wage is $22,500/month (USD 750)**. This is adjusted twice a year to account for inflation.

Once you have gotten a job, most companies will request a copy of your Uruguayan national ID (*Cédula de Identidad*), though some will accept just a passport. It's a good idea to clarify exactly what you will need after you have been offered the job to avoid delays in starting.

TAXES

There are various different taxes in Uruguay. The most relevan ones for most people will be VAT, income tax and property tax These are all collected by the DGI (*Dirección General Impostiva*) which has been linked below. We will go into more details o each kind of tax, but if you need more information, or t download any forms/paperwork you should check here:

www.dgi.gub.uy

Remember that you are only considered a tax resident in Urugua if you live there for more than 183 days in the year.

Value Added Tax (*Impuesto al Valor Agregado*)

VAT is 22% for most goods, though some products have a rate c only 10% or are VAT free. This tax is always added in to th advertised price, so you will never get a nasty shock at the cas register.

Another thing worth remembering is that VAT is reduced if yo pay with a debit card (4% less) – an easy way to save a fe pesos!
To find out more, take a look at the following link:

inclusionfinanciera.mef.gub.uy

Income Tax (*IRPF*)

Income tax, or IRPF, is paid by everyone earning over a certa amount every year. The tax-free minimum will vary year on ye ($26,936 – USD 900, in 2018). To find out how much you will ha to pay, take a look at the article below.

goo.gl/aG24Kc

IRPF is a progressive rate and ranges from between 0% and 36%. If you work in a company, this will be deducted monthly from your salary. If you work on a freelance basis, or have more than one job, you will need to calculate your own tax. Keep in mind that deductions are allowed for things like contributions to social security (*BPS*) or having a minor child.

Every year before December 31st, you will need to submit a return either personally at DGI or Abitab/Redpagos, or online. Here you will be able to find all of the paperwork you need to submit.

goo.gl/h2THMl

After you submit your return, you may to be asked to pay more tax to make up the balance, or if you are lucky, you will be granted a refund.

Remember that if you are married you can choose to file your taxes as an individual or with your nuclear family, so it's a good idea to do your sums and check which one is best for you.

If you pay your taxes late there will be a penalty of 5%, 10% or 15% plus a surcharge of 1% so it's best to get them in on time.

Until you get used to the Uruguayan tax system we recommend hiring a tax accountant to do your returns for you.

For recommendations on English speaking accountants, see the end of this section.

Social Security (*BPS*)

BPS is paid as a part of your salary every month. It contributes to things like healthcare and pensions. Both you and your employer will contribute to this every month. To calculate how much you will need to pay, use the calculator linked below.

goo.gl/m7CtRr

Property Tax (*Contribución Inmobiliaria*)

If you own a property you will have t pay tax of between 0.25% and 1.4% o the property value. The value of you property will be decided by th government. This tax is paid in variou instalments every year, and will b sent to your house in bill form.

goo.gl/exAZw9

School Tax (*Impuesto de Primaria*)

Another tax you may have to pay on your property is the school tax (*Impuesto de Primaria*). This will cost between 0.15% and 0.3% of the value of your house.

For more information on this, check the following link:

www.impuestoprimaria.edu.uy

Foreign Income

One of the many benefits of moving to Uruguay is that foreign incomes such as pensions, retirement income, lease income or capital gains are untaxed.

The only exception to this is income from dividends and interest. You will be exempt from paying tax on these for five years after you become a tax resident, though after that you will be required to pay income tax of 12%. However, if you pay more than 12% tax on this income in another country, you will not need to pay this tax in Uruguay. This is to avoid double taxation.

Corporate Income Tax

If you own a company, we recommend hiring a tax accountant to bring you through the ins and outs of Uruguayan corporate income tax and corporate taxation in general.

At a glance, the main income tax you will need to pay is called *IRAE*. This is paid by every company with residence in Uruguay, or with a permanent establishment there. The amount you will need to pay is 25% of net taxable income. To find out more about this, check the website linked below.

goo.gl/4uRnRX

For a full picture on corporate taxation have a look at some of the resources below.

goo.gl/YdzM5I EN/PT   **goo.gl/OXFhcd** EN

English Speaking Tax Accountants

www.fs.com.uy EN   **www.uhygubba.uy** EN
goo.gl/W1BNnN EN   **www.pkfuruguay.com.uy** EN

BANKS

Uruguay has a variety of banks to choose from, both in the public and private sector. Opening an account can be a little tricky, due to the wide range of documents required, so it's a good idea to come prepared, or you will be left feeling frustrated.

Banking in Uruguay is protected by secrecy laws, which may cause some problems for US citizens. Due to complicated procedures enforced by the IRS for US citizens living abroad, many Uruguayan banks will not accept US customers.

Uruguay's National Bank (*BROU*)

The bank we would recommend going with is the *Banco de l República Oriental del Uruguay* (BROU). This is the biggest bank in Uruguay and is state owned. It is also one of the only bank which accepts US customers.

For more information on BROU check the link below.

www.portal.brou.com.uy

Private Banks

There are also many private banks operating in Uruguay including HSBC, Scotiabank and Citibank, along with various private Uruguayan banks. For a list of banks have a look at the following link.

goo.gl/H8jTKq

Requirements for opening an Account

The following documents are needed for opening an account with BROU, but you will need these to open an account in most other banks too.

When going to open an account remember to bring both a photocopy and the original of your documents.

Please note that if you are using any foreign paperwork to open an account it should be translated into Spanish and legalised.

➡ **Two international forms of ID**
This can include your passport, your national ID (card format) or a driver's licence. If you have a Uruguayan ID this will be enough.

➡ **Proof of Residence**
This should be in the form of a utility bill issued in your name and should be less than 30 days old.

➡ **Proof of Income**
If you are an employee this will normally be your last payslip.

If you are a retiree, you should bring a proof of your pension.

If you are self-employed you will need to present a certificate of average monthly income (*Certificación de Ingresos Promedio Mensual*) made up by an accountant or public notary. These should also be notarised by the Chamber of Notaries (*Colegio de Escribanos*): **www.aeu.org.uy**

➡ **Minimum Deposit**
This is normally between USD 200 and USD 500 depending on what kind of account you're opening. The money does not necessarily need to be paid in cash; it can also be transferred from your home bank. Remember that if you are depositing more than USD 10,000 into an account you will have to bring proof of where the funds came from.

The bank may also ask for additional documents, but this is not so common.

ATMs

There are two branches of ATMs: **REDBROU** and **BANRED**. These can normally be found in shopping malls, big supermarkets, petrol stations, and of course in banks. REDBROU accepts the widest variety of cards, so if you are withdrawing from an international account, this is the branch you need to find.

Most ATMs are in English and Spanish, so there's no need to b worried about using them. They will also give you the optio between withdrawing in pesos or dollars. You will also get you cash before you finish the transaction, so make sure to finis your transaction and take your card before you leave.

Keep in mind that the ATMs only have a limited amount of mone inside, and will sometimes run out. This also means that th amount of money you can withdraw at a time will vary.

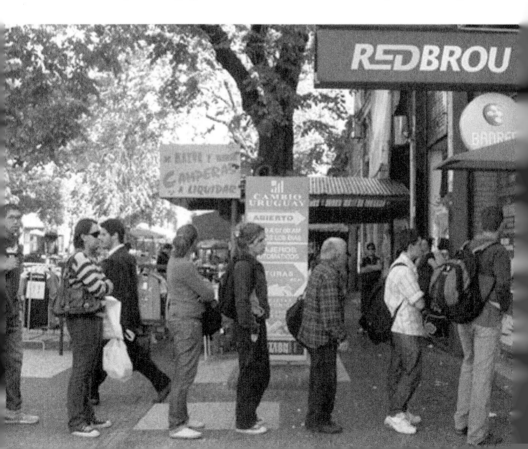

REVALIDATING YOUR DEGREE

If you are a professional with a degree from outside of Uruguay it is necessary to get it revalidated, unless you got it in Chile. There are two ways of doing this, depending on what country you come from.

For most people legalising a degree will involve getting an apostille stamp, however this option is not applicable for every nationality. For a full list of eligible countries check the link below.

goo.gl/SJMEfb

If you are not eligible for an apostille you can get your degree legalised by bringing the original to the closest Uruguayan Consulate in the country where the degree was issued. After your arrival you must then submit it to the Ministry of Foreign Affairs.

Once you have completed legalising your document, you can then submit it to the *Universidad de la República Uruguay* (University of the Republic of Uruguay), along with a letter to the Chancellor requesting the revalidation.

If you want to continue your studies in Uruguay it is worth checking if there is a link between your home university and the *Universidad de la República*, as there may already be an agreement in place.

Please remember that if your degree is not in Spanish, it must be translated by a registered translator in Uruguay.

For more information on the revalidation of a degree for specific fields, have a look at the link below.

goo.gl/z8mDBQ

Ministry of Foreign Affairs (MRREE)

Bureau of Consular Affairs
Cuareim 1384, Ground Floor
Tel: (598) 2902 1010 Internal: 2055, 3116, 3118 and 3123
Email: **consultas.web@mrree.gub.uy**
Montevideo, Uruguay

University of the Republic (Udelar)

Regulatory Procedures – Legalization Section
Av. 18 de Julio 1968, 1st Floor
Tel: (598) 2400 9203 - 2408 3129 Internal: 224
www.universidad.edu.uy
Montevideo, Uruguay

HOUSING

Finding the right place to live will probably be one of the bigger challenges you will face while making your move. There's a lot to be considered, such as where exactly in Uruguay you want to live, and what kind of lifestyle you plan on having.

While choosing, remember that towns in Uruguay are quite small. Most of the population is concentrated in Montevideo, so all other towns are considered the countryside.

To give you a hand in deciding, we have put together a location guide.

Location Guide

The departments that most expats choose to live in are Montevideo, Canelones, Maldonado, Colonia, Paysandú and Salto. Below we'll give a quick overview of prices you can expect to pay in each area, along with a brief description.

All of the prices quoted here are just reference points for the minimum you can expect to pay for unfurnished places, excluding bills.

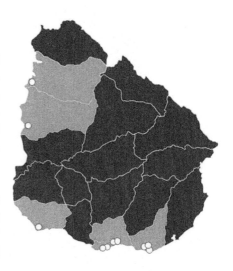

MONTEVIDEO

Montevideo is the capital and also the most populous city in Uruguay. If you don't already have a job going over, this is probably the best place for you to set up as it'll have the most opportunities. It also has the most varied options for joining activities such as gyms and clubs.

Remember though, that as it is the capital city, crime will be a little higher than if you live in the countryside, so you should choose your neighbourhood carefully.

The neighbourhoods that are most popular with expats are: Pocitos, Carrasco, Punta Carretas, Punta Gorda, Malvín, Buceo, Parque Batlle, Villa Dolores, Barrio Sur, Palermo, Parque Rodó and Centro.

These areas are relatively safe and well connected, though may seem a little on the expensive side with the minimum rent you can expect to pay being **USD 600** per month for an apartment of **40m²**.

CANELONES

Canelones is within commuting distance of Montevideo, and attracts a lot of people looking to escape the city. It is a lot greener and also safer than Montevideo. If you choose to live here, we would recommend getting a car, as public transport can be quite slow and crowded.

The areas most expats choose to live in are: Barra de Carrasco, El Pinar and Lomas de Solymar.

To get somewhere here you can expect to pay a minimum of **US 500** per month for a house of **40m²**.

COLONIA

Colonia is just across the river from Buenos Aires, making it a very popular tourist destination. The city that most expats choose to live in is Colonia del Sacramento. The old town is a world heritage site, and the people who live there are more used to foreigners, which is also a bonus for a lot of expats.

To rent a place in Colonia del Sacramento you can expect to pay a minimum of **USD 500** per month for a house of **40m²**.

MALDONADO

Maldonado is located along the coast, and is a popular holiday destination in the summer. The main areas people live in are Maldonado city, Punta del Este and Pinares/Las Delicias. Many Uruguayans view these areas as resort destinations, which means that the towns can be empty in winter. Nevertheless they remain popular amongst expats looking to live in close proximity to the beach.

This area is a little more expensive than the others, costing a minimum of **USD 600** per month for a house or an apartment of 40m².

PAYSANDÚ

Paysandú is located in northern Uruguay just across from Argentina and attracts expats looking for a more rural way of life. The city is more relaxed and the people are generally friendlier. The cost of life is also lower than in the other areas though the choice of things to do is also lower than in Montevideo.

To get somewhere in Paysandú you can expect to pay at least **USD 400** per month for a house of **40m²**.

SALTO

Salto is very similar to Paysandú. It is also located in the north of the country and is famous for its thermal waters. The cost of life is also similar to Paysandú and so is the standard of living.

To rent somewhere in Salto expect a minimum of **USD 400** per month for a house of **40m²**.

Although some people prefer living in areas that only Uruguayans live in, we would recommend staying somewhere more frequented by expats, unless you are really committed to adopting the Uruguayan way of life. It can feel very isolating at the beginning if you never meet someone from a similar cultural background to yourself, particularly if you have never been exposed to Uruguayan culture before.

Getting Started

Before committing to an area we recommend that you spend a little time there first. Check the commuting time to your work and make sure there are leisure activities that you enjoy close by. Uruguay has many well priced hotels and hostels to stay in until you get your bearings. Signing a long term lease and discovering that you don't like the area where you live is not a good way to begin your life abroad.

Below are links to find hotels and hostels. Try and find one as close as possible to the area you want to live in.

Hotels: **www.booking.com**
www.hotelscombined.com

Hostels: **www.airbnb.com**
www.hostelworld.com

If you are on a budget and can't afford a hotel or a hostel you can also use types of accommodation more traditionally used by travellers and backpackers. Just remember that living in this kind of accommodation with a suitcase full of everything you might need for the next year may not be the most stress free experience.

Couchsurfing: **www.couchsurfing.org**

Farms: **www.wwoofindependents.org**

If you would like to have somewhere a bit more permanent arranged before you go, short term apartments are also an excellent option. Short term apartments can normally be rented on a month to month basis and will provide a base for you to find a job and get to know your area before committing to anything long term. They are however substantially more expensive than long term arrangements, so you'll need to allow for that in your budget. Before you pay a deposit, make sure you have viewed the place in person and to get a receipt after each transaction.

www.rentinuruguay.com EN

goo.gl/5kMRfi EN

www.rentahome.com.uy EN

goo.gl/11WRh8 EN

www.01montevideouruguay.com EN

Long Term Living

Whether buying or renting in Uruguay, you'll have your work cut out for you as both require a lot of paperwork. In this section we'll provide you with an overview of the formalities of both buying and renting.

Below we have listed what we consider to be the most useful websites for finding long term leases or houses to buy. While looking, keep in mind that apartments and houses come completely unfurnished – as in without kitchen cabinets or even a toilet seat – so you'll need to factor the cost of furniture into your budget.

www.gallito.com.uy/inmuebles

www.buscandocasa.com

www.mercadolibre.com.uy/inmuebles

www.casas.com.uy

Shared apartments are not so common in Uruguay, though there are some options, particularly for students:

goo.gl/TuHcdj

goo.gl/GcZXlY

Offers will also sometimes be posted in the following **Facebook groups**:

goo.gl/uYnzVT

goo.gl/7jdUVJ

Estate agents (*Inmobiliarias*) are another good way to find somewhere to live, especially if you are thinking of buying a house. Remember that they charge a commission, so don't forget to include that in your budget.

As there are so many estate agents across Uruguay we recommend putting **inmobiliaria + the neighbourhood or city that you are looking for** into Google and check where they are on the map.

Alternatively you can also check this website, which has a full list of estate agents across the whole country.

ciu.org.uy/asociados/

Rental Guarantees

Renting can be a little complicated in Uruguay, as most places require a guarantee (*Garantía de Alquiler*) instead of a deposit. Here we will explain briefly how both ways work.

DEPOSITS

As mentioned, a deposit is not a common form of payment, though if you've just arrived, it is the easiest choice. Paying with a deposit involves leaving 4 – 6 months' rent in trust in a bank account set up by the landlord, for the duration of your contract. You should receive all of this money back at the end. Before you agree to rent somewhere, make sure the landlord is happy to accept a deposit, as most would only prefer a guarantee.

GUARANTEES (*Garantías de Alquiler*)

A guarantee is issued either by the state or a private company. It is similar to paying insurance, in that you pay a fixed amount at the beginning, and the company will pay out if you break your contract with the landlord. It's also important to note that most companies will only cover you for a rent of up to 30% of your net salary.

Although the fixed fee you pay is non-refundable, most Uruguayans prefer this method as it means they don't have a large amount of money tied up in the bank. For example for a one year guarantee on somewhere with a monthly rent of $15,000 (USD 500), you may only need to pay a fixed fee of

$12,000 (USD 400). This is a lot more affordable than the $90,000 (USD 3,000) you'd be expected to pay for the deposit.

The best way to get a guarantee is to go through a private company. However as most companies will want to be certain that you can afford to pay if anything goes wrong, they will carry out stringent checks on your financial situation.

Some examples of documents you might need are your Uruguayan ID (*Cédula*), along with your last 3 payslips or bank statement for the previous 12 months. Keep in mind that some companies will only provide guarantees to people who have been living and working in Uruguay for over a year, though some will also accept a guarantor to help you to make up the requirements. To find out exactly what you need, it's best to get in contact with the company, as each will have different requirements.

Once you have received your guarantee, the company will give you a document to present to the landlord.

GUARANTEE PROVIDERS

The following is a list of private guarantee providers in Uruguay

goo.gl/Bd6xJh
goo.gl/hMVaQ9
www.fideciu.uy

The state also provides guarantees, though they are geared more toward people with a lower income. MVOTMA is one of the organisations which provides these guarantees. The financial checks are tough, and are aimed more at people who have been living in Uruguay for a long time. For more information on the requirements, check the link below.

goo.gl/14SCnw

SGA also provides state guarantees, but only for public employees, and employees of specific private companies. To see if this applies to your company, check the link below.

goo.gl/gbfqMc

Buying a House

Buying a house is relatively straightforward. Once your offer for the house has been accepted, you must contact a notary (*escribano*) to get the paperwork in order. To find a notary, follow the link below:

www.aeu.org.uy

Next your notary will organise a preliminary sales contract (*Boleto de Reserva*), which should contain all the details of the sale. At this point you will also have to pay a deposit (normally around 10%), which will be held in trust by the notary.

Following that, the notary will gather all the documents needed to ensure that there are no legal issues preventing the sale of the property. Once this has been cleared, both you and the seller will sign the final transfer deed (*Escritura de Compraventa*) and you will pay the outstanding amount. The notary will then record the purchase in the property registry, and the house will be yours. Along with the blueprints, you will also be provided with the history of the house going back 30 years.

Keep in mind that you must also pay taxes on the purchase price. The total tax will amount to 14% of the price, though you will not be responsible for paying all of it. You should only have to pay 9% and the seller will make up the other 5%. The notary will pay this while registering your property, so you don't need to worry about it.

Things to take note of:

➡ Refuse is normally collected by the city from big bins located on the street in each neighbourhood. This means you don't need to pay anything for collection.

➡ As security is a big concern amongst most Uruguayans don't be surprised if the windows of your house have bars and the property is surrounded by a fence. This is normal and does not reflect the quality of the neighbourhood.

➡ Each household in Uruguay is responsible for maintaining its own sewage system, which means that at some point you will need to clean your grease trap. Many people hire someone to do this for them, but it is easy to do yourself. If you don't clean it often enough it will begin to smell especially during the summer.

Things to watch out for:

➡ We cannot stress enough that apartments and houses come completely unfurnished – as in without even a toilet seat. This also goes for cookers and kitchen cabinets. Rent only pays for the privilege of having a roof. Everything else you need to supply yourself.

➡ A lot of buildings are poorly insulated, which can result in high heating bills in the winter. Similarly air conditioning costs in the summer will also be quite high.

➡ Mould can be a big problem in some houses due to the high humidity, so it's always a good idea to check for signs of mould before you make your decision.

➡ Make sure to check that the water in the kitchen runs at the same time as the water in the bathroom as sometimes there can be a problem with water pressure.

CONNECTING UTILITIES

Connecting utilities like water, electricity, internet, cable TV and gas is pretty straightforward. Most services will already be connected, so you'll just need to change the name on the account.

Electricity

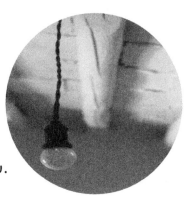

The only electricity provider in Uruguay is **UTE**. To change the name on the account in your home, it's best to visit one of their shops. While you don't need an appointment, it's a good idea to make one to avoid queues. To find a shop near you visit the link below.

goo.gl/y4bO3F

To change the name on the account you will need a valid national ID (*Cédula*) and the last bill paid. Make sure to ask for this bill while you're making the changeover from the previous tenant.

Water

To transfer the water account you'll need to go to an **OSE** service centre. To find one near you, follow the link below.

goo.gl/yhRNLE

You'll need to bring a valid ID, and a document which shows your connection with the property e.g. the property deed, rental contract or a utility bill. You may also be asked to sign a sworn statement saying that the property is yours/is being rented by you.

If none of these are ok, you will be asked to go to get the registration number of the house (*Número de Padrón*) from the

Property Registry (*Catastro*). This is not so common, but if you need to request it, follow the link below to find your nearest office.

goo.gl/d4Q8hk

Gas

Connecting up to gas can be a little complicated, as the gas installation pipe coverage in the country is quite limited.

If you live in Montevideo check the link below to see if your home is over the gas pipe network.

goo.gl/DhrjPm

If your house has coverage, contact **Montevideo Gas** to request connection. The best way to get in contact is to phone them, but you can also send an email, or visit their commercial centre in Ciudad Vieja.

To get in contact, or to find out more information on the services, follow the link below.

goo.gl/wBUL8J

If you live outside Montevideo, you'll need to get in contact with **Conecta**. They'll be able to tell you if your house has pipe coverage or not, and help you to get set up.

To find out more information, check the following link:

www.conecta.com.uy

If you do not have pipe coverage, don't worry. Gas canisters are cheap and easy to get. For 13 kg of gas you can normally expect to pay around $565 (USD 19), though if you do not already own a canister you will also need to buy one. These normally cost around $2,290 (USD 76), but are a once off purchase.

The most popular companies for buying gas canisters are:

www.acodike.com.uy   **www.megal.uy**

Internet

There are lots of different options for internet, ranging from pre-paid sticks to contracts with unlimited usage.

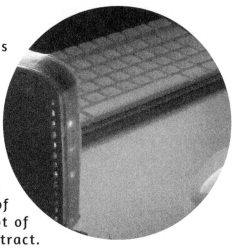

If you're looking for a quick solution, a pre-paid stick is the way to go. To use one of these you don't need to sign any contracts or produce any proof of address, however if you use a lot of internet, it's worth getting a contract.

We've listed the main internet providers below. We recommend checking through them to find the best deal for you. Most contracts will come with a data limit, so make sure you have enough, as the extra charges can be quite high.

www.antel.com.uy   **www.dedicado.com.uy**
www.claro.com.uy   **www.movistar.com.uy**
conecta.montevideo.com.uy   **netgate.uy**

Television

In Uruguay there are various stations available for free. Each department has their own channels, but the main four from Montevideo are also available in most of the other departments. These channels are very popular, but are only in Spanish. To get these just plug in your TV and watch.

If you're looking for some TV channels in English or another language, you'll need to get cable. Each company will offer different deals and different packages, so it's best to shop around. Getting cable is generally not too expensive, but most companies will ask you to sign an unbreakable two year contract, so make sure you really want it.

Below we have listed the main companies, though you will also find some smaller, local companies outside of Montevideo.

www.cableplus.com.uy   www.montecable.com

www.cablevision.com.uy   www.tcc.com.uy

www.directv.com.uy   www.nuevosiglo.com.uy

Landline

Landlines are still really common in Uruguay, so it's a good idea to have one. **Antel** is the company that deals with landlines. Remember that a landline service can also be bundled with the internet, so have a good look at all of their deals. To find out information on their prices check the following link:

www.antel.com.uy

To transfer the account for your home to your name, follow the link below and fill out the online form. You will need to get the service and account number from the previous tenant, so make sure to ask them during the handover. These numbers can be found easily on the bill.

goo.gl/LYyXVQ

Making international calls from a landline can be expensive so we recommend using Skype or Facebook calls. Both of the services are free and can be used on your mobile phone.

In Uruguay electricity operates at 220 volts.

To make things complicated, there are four kinds of plug: the **L** model, the **Schuko**, the **C** model and the **I** model.

The **L** model is the most common kind of socket, though the **Schuko** and the **C** socket are also common. The **I** model is on its way to becoming obsolete and can only be found in older establishments.

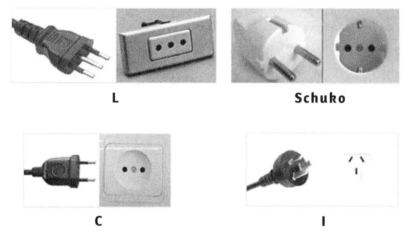

L   Schuko

C   I

You will not know what kind of sockets you will have in your new home, until you find it, but don't worry, adaptors are easy to come by in hardware shops (*ferretería*) and electrical goods stores. We recommend coming over with an **L** model adaptor to tide you over until you find out what kind you'll need for your new home.

EVERYDAY SHOPS

Shops to suit your everyday needs are ten a penny. You'll find an abundance of greengrocers, butchers, bakeries and corner shops. Small business are the norm for day-to-day use, though you'll also find plenty of supermarkets for weekly shopping or for household needs. In this section we'll go through the most common kinds of shops for food, furniture, clothes and knick-knacks.

Food Shopping

Shopping for food is something that you will normally do on weekly basis in Uruguay and as food prices are quite high, yo may have to go to more than one shop to keep your shoppin bills relatively low.

Supermarkets are a great place to get the bulk of your shoppin done. The most common and affordable chains are:

www.devoto.com.uy   **www.disco.com.uy**

www.multiahorro.com.uy   **www.tata.com.uy**

If you live in Maldonado, you can also add **El Dorado** to this lis

www.eldorado.com.uy

Macromercado is the most popular choice amongst Uruguaya for bulk shopping as they offer huge discounts for bulk buyin Here you can get almost anything including some househo items.

www.macromercado.com.uy

Tienda Inglesa is more expensive than the other chains, thou it does have a good selection of imported goods. It is also t best bet if you're missing something from home, as every so often they have products with a theme from a different country, which adds a nice variety to the weekly shop.

www.tinglesa.com.uy

Geant is located in Canelones, near the border with Montevideo. It is the biggest supermarket in Uruguay and also sells goods like clothes and books, along with food.

www.geant.com.uy

To find which supermarket carries the cheapest items, check the website below.

www.precios.uy

Corner shops should also not be overlooked while doing your shopping. Here you can get basics such as bread, milk, rice, pasta and sometimes even some fruit and vegetables. Most neighbourhoods will also have a bakery and a newsagent. These are a little more expensive than supermarkets, but the convenience makes up for the price. Though corner shops require a lot more interaction with the shopkeeper, they are also a good way to get to know your neighbours, so don't be afraid to use them!

Bills, Tickets and Scratch Cards

For paying bills, buying scratch cards or buying concert tickets, **Redpagos** and **Abitab** are the shops you need to go to. Both are pretty common, so you shouldn't have a problem locating one near you.

www.redpagos.com.uy   www.abitab.com.uy

Mobile Phones

Acquiring a working mobile phone should be one of your first priorities in Uruguay. Being easily reachable is one of the most important factors in finding a home or a job.

The easiest way to go about this is to get your phone unblocked before you leave, and pick up a new sim card once you arrive. Just remember that you need to declare your phone in the airport customs after you fly in.

There are 3 main network providers in Uruguay:

antel.com.uy   movistar.com.uy   claro.com.uy

Antel and **Movistar** are the two biggest companies, though competition between all of them is pretty fierce, so shop around for the best deals.

When you've just arrived, buying a prepaid sim card is your best option as you don't need any documents. Just go to the shop and ask for a *"chip prepago"*. Sometimes you will also get asked for an ID when buying a sim card, so make sure to bring one along just in case.

You can buy phone credit at any newsagent, petrol station or in an **Abitab** or **RedPagos**. To get phone credit ask for a *"recarga"*, tell the shop assistant your phone network and give them your number. If you're not confident with numbers in Spanish, just write it down on a piece of paper and hand it to them.

62

Once you get your feet on the ground, you may also want to think about setting up a monthly contract. Although these can be much cheaper than pre-paid phones, you will also need to be sure that you are staying for a year, as you cannot break the contract. To sign up for a contract just bring a proof of address (normally a utility bill), proof of income and also your Uruguayan ID to a phone shop near you and ask for a *"contrato mensual"*.

Internet Cafes (Cibercafés)

Internet cafes are becoming less and less popular in Uruguay as most people have laptops and smart phones. Nevertheless, if you need one, you won't be long looking. For more specific locations check out the website below.

www.cybercafes.com

Printing, Photo IDs and Photocopies

Printing and photocopying are cheap and easy to do in Uruguay. Most newsagents, and of course internet cafes will be able to provide these services.

ID photos are also available at a lot of newsagents or shops where they sell cameras. Just ask for a *"foto carnet"*.

Post Offices

In theory, sending and receiving post isn't too difficult. Letters can be posted in post offices, or in most pharmacies, and you will receive them in your letter box at home.

Parcels can also be sent in this way and will also be brought to your house when you receive one. If you are not at home, don't worry, you will get a note through the door, telling you which post office it's been left in. All you need to do is bring your ID and the post slip and pick it up. Simple, right?

Unfortunately things get complicated if you are receiving packages with expensive goods. If you receive something by **non express mail**, you will need to pay taxes on anything worth more than USD 50.

For **express mail (EMS)** the limit is USD 200. If you exceed this you will need to hire a customs agent, as it will be treated as an importation. Please keep in mind that these regulations change constantly, so to make sure you have the most up-to-date information, check the link below.

goo.gl/gpaSEy

For more general information check the *Correo Uruguayo* website. Remember, if in doubt, always ask at the post office.

www.correo.com.uy

Home Shopping

Shopping for your home can be time consuming and expensive. There isn't too much of a choice if you're looking for a one stop furniture shop like **Ikea**, which means that furnishing your house may take a lot longer than you'd planned.

One of the biggest furniture shops is called **Divino**. This is located in Montevideo, Canelones, Salto, Paysandú and Maldonado and is probably the best point of reference for planning your budget.

www.divino.com.uy

Sodimac is another good option. This can be found near Geant supermarket on the border of Canelones and Montevideo and also in Sayago inside Montevideo.

www.sodimac.com.uy

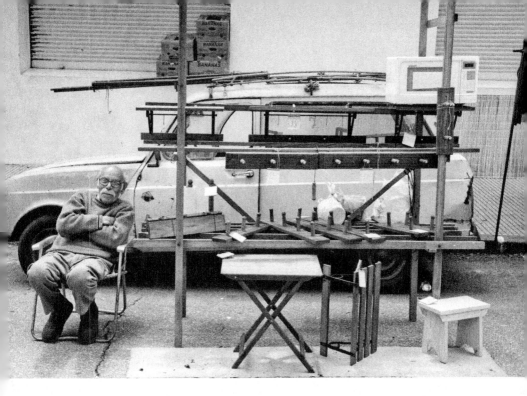

There are also numerous small shops and stalls dotted around the different cities in Uruguay. You may even spot some furniture being sold at the side of the road.

If don't fancy going shopping you can also commission furniture from a **carpenter's shop** (*carpintería*). All you need is to have a rough budget and an idea of what you want, and the carpenter will do the rest. Surprisingly, this is a very affordable option and a lot of Uruguayans choose this option. To try and find a carpenter near you, have a look at the listings linked below.

goo.gl/Sbavle

For **homeware**, a lot of supermarkets sell decent quality items at good prices. You'll also find small homeware shops scattered around your city, as you get to know the area better – It's a long process.

To get **electronics** most Uruguayans visit **Carlos Gutiérrez** in Montevideo. It's one of the most popular shops for electrical goods in the country and is well worth a visit.

www.carlosgutierrez.com.uy

Markets (*Ferias*)

Montevideo is full of markets, ranging from small neighbourhood markets to huge ones spanning streets.
Neighbourhood markets will normally specialise in food, such as vegetables, fish, cheese and fruit, while in the bigger ones you can also find books, clothes, antiques and toys.

The main market in Montevideo is the Mercado Agrícola. This also has the best selection of **fruit and vegetables**.

goo.gl/m1Pk7d

If you're looking for **antiques**, the *Feria de la Plaza de l Constitución* in Ciudad Vieja is your best bet.

For **clothes** check either *Feria de Villa Biarritz* in Pocitos/Punt Carretas, or *Feria de Parque Rodó* in Parque Rodó.

If you're looking for a **flea market**, *Feria de Tristán Narvaja* i Centro is the place to go.

While in the market always keep a half an eye on your bag an pockets, as a lot of pickpockets operate in these areas.

You may also see people playing the shell game (where you hau three identical cups and a ball, and shuffle them around particularly at the *Feria de Tristán Narvaja*. This game is illeg in Uruguay, and is mostly used to scam people. If you even star around to watch, you may leave with your pockets lighter, so u recommend just ignoring it.

Shopping Malls

Uruguay is not exactly famous for its shopping opportunitie and though there are many malls arounds, you might find th the choice in them is quite limited. Aside from shops, most ma also have a **cinema** and of course a **food court**.

The highest concentration of malls is in Montevideo. They are scattered all over the city and each has something different to offer. To find which one you'd like to visit, browse through the links to the right.

www.trescruces.com.uy
www.montevideoshopping.com.uy
www.puntacarretas.com.uy
www.nuevocentroshopping.com.uy
www.portones.com.uy

If you're outside Montevideo, you can also visit Canelones and Maldonado to find big shopping malls. If you live anywhere else, you'll most likely need to do shopping the old fashioned way – by walking around the town centre.

CANELONES	MALDONADO
www.costaurbana.com.uy	www.puntashopping.com.uy

Clothes Shopping

Clothes are expensive in Uruguay, so this is not something you will want to do too often. Most Uruguayans wear what they have until it can't possibly be used anymore as there are no cheap alternatives.

Most new clothes are bought in clothes shops in malls, or at markets.

Second Hand Shopping

Uruguayans don't like to throw things away, so there are plenty of things to be bought second hand. **Markets** are a great place to do some second hand shopping, though vendors there will mostly be selling antiques.

For more modern goods and clothes the best place to look is the website **Mercadolibre**, which is full of items, both new and used, at great prices.

www.mercadolibre.com.uy

LOCAL ENTERTAINMENT

Uruguayans work very hard during the week and use the weekend to relax. As a result there's not a lot on during the week, particularly during winter when people prefer to watch TV at home or go to the gym. In summer there's a little more on as people like to go to a park, walk by the coast, or simply sit in their garden and spend the evening drinking *mate*. Weekends are much busier, with things such as festivals, concerts and games taking place on a regular basis. For more information on what's going on, check the event guides linked below.

www.culturayeventos.uy

www.cartelera.com.uy

goo.gl/r1yua3

Eating Out

Many expats find the restaurant choices in Uruguay pret limited. If you're not a fan of meat and fast food, you might fir yourself in trouble, and although Uruguayan food has heav Italian and Spanish influences, international cuisine is not te easy to come by. Restaurants are normally found on main stree but small bars can be found in every neighbourhood.

Before you go out, remember that lunch is normally serv between 12.00 and 15.00 and dinner is normally eaten betwe 20.00 and 23.00. If you don't eat during those times, you mig find your choice of restaurants severely limited.

STREET FOOD

Food stalls (*carritos*) are mainly aimed at people looking for something to eat after a night out or during rush hour. They normally sell hot dogs (*panchos*), hamburgers (*hamburguesas*) and sausages in bread (*chorizos al pan*). The food is not of the highest quality, but is nevertheless very popular.

FAST FOOD

Fast food is very affordable, and many Uruguayans eat it for lunch during the week. Traditional fast food is the most popular, with many people choosing to fill up on things like tarts, *empanadas* (pastries filled with meat, cheese or vegetables), *chivitos* (beef sandwich with eggs, ham, cheese, French fries and salad), *milanesas* (breaded meat) or *fainá* (chickpea flatbread). Most bakeries prepare lunch time menus, where you can grab something quick, and there are also lots of local restaurants around to choose from. International food chains are also popular, but not as easy to find.

After work many locals also like to eat take away food. To see if you can find something you like check this website:

www.pedidosya.com.uy

PARRILLADAS (GRILL HOUSES)

Barbequed meat in all shapes and sizes is the national food of Uruguay and there are plenty of restaurants where you can find this. Most of these have an inside barbeque where they cook the meat over a wood fire. Every part of the cow is used, giving the diner a varied selection of cuts. In fact according to locals, the only part of the cow that isn't used is the moo!

The **Mercado del Puerto** is the most popular place to get an introduction to a *parrillada* restaurant, but it's really only used by tourists. Because of this the prices there will be much higher than in any other place.

INTERNATIONAL and VEGETARIAN RESTAURANTS

Uruguay is not very cosmopolitan, however there are some options for international dining. In Montevideo you can find these kind of restaurants mainly in Ciudad Vieja, Pocitos, Centro, Punta Carretas, Parque Rodó, Carrasco and Buceo.
If you are a vegetarian finding somewhere to eat out is not going to be easy. However if you live in Montevideo, you can find vegetarian restaurants in the neighbourhoods mentioned above. For listings of different restaurants, check the website below:

www.restaurantmontevideo.com EN/PT

CAFES

Cafes and coffee chains are not popular, but a few can be found in big shopping areas. Bars and confectionery shops are more common, and are also places where you can stop, get a pastry and drink a coffee.

BEERS, WINES and SPIRITS

The national beers in Uruguay are called Patricia and Pilsen. They are very popular and can be found in every shop and bar. Whisky is also very popular, with Johnny Walker being the drink of choice for many.
There are also many excellent wines to be found in Uruguay. **Tannat** is the national wine, and is not very common around the world. Vineyards can be found in almost every department, though they are mostly concentrated in Canelones, Montevideo, Colonia and San José.
Grappamiel is the national spirit. It's a kind of grappa mixed with honey and water, and can be drunk at room temperature or on ice. It's very popular to cool you down in the summer, to warm you up in the winter.

Another popular drink is the **Medio y Medio**. It's a blend made dry white wine and sweet sparkling wine, and is very refreshing in the summer.

Nightlife

Nightlife is mainly consigned to Fridays and Saturdays, and mostly consists of nightclubs, although pubs are also popular. Clubs start after midnight, though normally only fill up between 1 am and 1.30 am, and then close at around 6 am. Make sure to take care while you're out, as it's common for small fights to break out. Each club will attract a different clientele, so it's a good idea to ask around for recommendations.

Pubs and clubs can be found in every city. Most popular ones play music such as **cumbia** and *plena*, but it is possible to find other kinds of music too, particularly in more touristy areas.

Traditional Festivals and Events

Uruguayans celebrate a lot of traditional festivals throughout the year. Many of them take place on public holidays, so it's easy for everyone to take part.

The most important party of the year is the *Noche de la Nostalgia*, which is celebrated every year on the 24th of August. It originally started as a private party to celebrate old hits and has now become a national-wide celebration of music from the 70's right through to the 90's.

CARNAVAL

The most important festival is Carnaval, which runs from the end of January to the end of February or beginning of March. Uruguayan Carnaval originated from the European tradition, but has since evolved to take on its own distinctive traits. At 40 days long, it is also the longest carnival celebration in the world.

Carnaval consists of a series of shows, performed by different types of groups, such as *murgas*, *parodistas* and *humoristas*.

A *murga* is a chorus who sing about topical events affectin
Uruguay. They are often political, and heavily satirical. They ar
by far the most important kind of performers in Carnava
Parodistas on the other hand, create a dance-fuelled skit base
on books or films, while *humoristas* make you laugh with the
own creations.

To find out more, take a look at the link below.

www.carnavaldeluruguay.com

Another important part of Carnaval is the *Desfile de Llamada*
This is one of the most popular events, with tourists coming fro
all over to witness it. It is split into two days and involves for
drumming groups taking to the street, playing a kind of mus
called *candombe*.

RODEO

Jineteadas or *domas*, is a riding
discipline where the rider has to
stay on top of a wild horse for a
determined amount of time
without falling. This competition is
very popular during Easter week
and during the September holidays
in Montevideo. However, you can
find less professional and more
authentic *jineteadas* or *pruebas de
rienda* all around the country
during different times of the year.

The **Fiesta de la Patria Gaucha** is a celebration of traditional Uruguayan culture, where you find events such as *jineteadas* and folk music. It's held every year in Tacuarembó during the first few days of March.

www.patriagaucha.com.uy

EASTER WEEK

If you're around Paysandú, the **Semana de la Cerveza** is a popular beer festival held during Easter week. For more information on this, check the link below.

goo.gl/nZv3Cw

For more information on festivals around Uruguay, have a look at these websites:

www.fiestasuruguayas.com.uy   goo.gl/ZYkfoq

Outdoor Activities

PARKS

Green areas in Uruguay are not difficult to find. The cities are full of parks and squares, while the countryside is vast and green.

BEACHES

Beaches are also a common feature of the landscape along the many kilometres of ocean and river coast. The beaches are of a high standard, and are very popular. Before you go swimming, make sure to check the flag on the beach to see if the water is safe or not.

Sports

Uruguay has a thriving sports culture, with football taking top place as the national sport, and basketball coming in second. The best way to get involved is to pick a team and support it, as there is so much choice for both of these

sports. If you like something different, check our **Social and Hobbies** section and follow the links provided to find out more about teams and competition times.

Movies and Books

If you are missing the movies, Uruguay has various **cinemas** in malls all over the country. Generally speaking movies are screened in Spanish, but you can find some of them in English with Spanish subtitles. To avoid any mix ups make sure to check the language of the film on the cinema's website before booking anything.

www.cinemateca.org.uy   www.lifecinemas.com.uy
www.grupocine.com.uy   www.movie.com.uy

If you want to read we suggest purchasing an **e-reader** and getting **e-books** online in whatever language you want. While there are bookshops and libraries in Uruguay, most reading materials will be in Spanish. That being said, there are books available in English, just not with a great amount of choice. You will find bookshops on main avenues and in shopping centres.

Cultural Activities

Uruguay has a multitude of cultural activities. Theatres can found in abundance and museums are alive and well.
The National Auditorium, in particular, offers a rich mix of shows and cultural activities.

www.auditorio.com.uy

MUSEUMS

Museums will probably be the first port of call for many looking to learn a little more about their new home, and Uruguay will not disappoint. Whether you are interested in art, football or history this country will have it covered. Some museums will have an entrance fee, but other ones can be visited for free. To find museums of interest to you have a look at the link below.

museos.montevideo.gub.uy

THE THEATRE

If you are looking to discover Uruguay's plays, there are many options. Each department has plenty of theatres, though of course Montevideo has the most variety.
Follow the link below to find the addresses of all theatres in Uruguay.

goo.gl/gfoPzB

If you're looking for something extra special, the **Solís Theatre**, is the oldest in Uruguay. Although the plays are in Spanish the spectacle will be worth sitting through.

www.teatrosolis.org.uy EN

THE NATIONAL BALLET

If you are interested in ballet the Sodre National Ballet is the only real option in Uruguay.

www.balletnacionalsodre.gub.uy EN

CLASSICAL MUSIC

For classical music the Montevideo Philharmonic Orchestra is a good choice for an evening out without the need of Spanish.

orquestafilarmonica.montevideo.gub.uy

Tours

Taking a tour in Montevideo can be a good way to get to know several different areas and discover the importance of different buildings. There are three kinds of tour to be found: walking tours, bus tours and helicopter tours.

WALKING TOURS

Walking tours will bring you to all the major tourist attraction over the period of a day, along with outlining the history an significance of what you are seeing. The Free Walking Tour is ti based, so make sure to pay your guide what you think the tou was worth.

www.freewalkingtour.com.uy EN

If you are interested in **Jewish history**, the following tour wi take you through the origins of the Uruguayan Jewish communi

www.jewishexp.com EN/PT

If pub culture is more your thing, this **pub crawl** based Montevideo is a sure thing.

www.pubcrawlmontevideo.com EN

Of course no tour of Montevideo would be complete witho getting to know more about **Uruguayan football**. Fanátic Fútbol Tours will have you covered on this front.

www.futboltours.com.uy EN

BUS TOURS

As with the walking tour, the bus tour will bring you to eve major tourist attraction, and allow you time to get off a explore the different locations. The prices are fixed, and day passes are available.

Bus Turístico Montevideo will bring you right through the ins and outs of Montevideo.

www.busturisticomontevideo.com.uy EN/PT

Alternatively if you are traveling to Colonia from Buenos Aires for the day, **Bus Turístico** is a good option.

www.buquebus.com/colonia EN/DE/PT

HELICOPTER TOURS

A helicopter tour offers you panoramic views of Montevideo and Punta del Este and let you experience the diversity of Uruguay from above.

www.turismoexcellence.com EN/FR

Sight-Seeing

In Uruguay sight-seeing is largely made up of outdoor activities and going to the beach. However, there are a lot of places to visit all around the country, even if you're not near the water.

MONTEVIDEO

Castillo Pittamiglio is a creative space built by the alchemist Humberto Pittamiglio. The façade is in the shape of a ship and the inside is just as weird and wonderful. There is an entrance fee and a guided tour.

www.castillopittamiglio.org

Mercado de la Abundancia is an artisane market place, where many tourists go to find traditional Uruguayan food, and handmade crafts. If you're lucky you may even get to witness a tango show. This is a little on the expensive side, but well worth a look if you want to treat yourself.

ROCHA

Cabo Polonio is an ocean-side village, located in a protecte
natural area. This means that there is no electricity and very fe
buildings are built to last. The area is famous for its seals an
wild natural beauty.

www.portaldelcabo.com.uy EN/PT

SAN JOSÉ

The **Barrancas de Kiyú** are located in the south of Uruguay o
the *Río de la Plata* (River Plate). It has been made famous by th
discovery of dinosaur fossils in its long strip of cliffs. Th
naturalist Darwin also visited this area during his expedition t
South America.

SALTO and PAYSANDÚ

Acuamania is a waterpark located in Salto. It's chock full
water slides and swimming pools, and is a great day out for a
the family.

www.acuamania.com.uy

Paysandú and Salto are also famous for their **thermal wate**
(*aguas termales*). There are various resorts and baths all ov
both departments.

MALDONADO

Maldonado is most famous for the city of **Punta del Este**. Golden beaches and designer shops make it a magnet for wealthier tourists. Some high points in the area include the **Fingers of Punta del Este** (a sculpture in the town centre) and the **Parque El Jagüel** (an outdoor adventure park for kids).

If you're looking for somewhere which is more frequented by Uruguayan holiday makers, **Piriápolis** is a great option. The beaches are just as beautiful as in Punta del Este, but the atmosphere is much more relaxed. The clientele are more middle class, which is reflected in the prices in the shops around.
If you're in the area **Piria's Castle** is also well worth a look. This residence was completed in 1897 for Francisco Piria and blends a spectrum of styles, from classical to medieval.

TACUAREMBÓ

San Gregorio de Polanco is an idyllic beach resort, surrounded by natural beauty. It is popular amongst fishing enthusiasts as has an abundance of mackerel, catfish and wolf-fish.

TREINTA Y TRES

Quebrada de los Cuervos is a beautiful gorge in an isolated part of Treinta y Tres. It is ideal for adventure tourists looking to get to know the wilder side of Uruguay.

FLORES

Grutas del Palacio (Palace Cave) is a geopark comprising of pillars made out of sandstone, which look quite similar to ruined columns in a palace. It is currently being considered by **UNESCO** to become a world heritage site due to its geological importance.

ARTIGAS

Artigas is famous for its semi-precious stones, such as amethyst and agate. Though not strictly open to tourists, quarry staff are generally happy to give you a tour if you show interest.

COLONIA

The **historic quarter of Colonia del Sacramento** dates back to 1680, and is now a **UNESCO** world heritage site. The cobbled streets and colourful houses inside this riverside fort provide a poignant reminder of Uruguay's Spanish and Portuguese colonial past. Inside the city there is an abundance of museums and activities.

If you're looking for more sights to see in Uruguay, or information on the areas we've covered, this government website is full of information about protected areas.

www.mvotma.gub.uy/snap

SOCIAL AND HOBBIES

Making friends and socialising in a new country can be daunting for anyone; however Uruguay is well set up for this task. With clubs, societies and an active ex-pat community, it is not difficult to start getting to know people and making new friends.

Social

To ease this process we recommend joining an expat group before you arrive. Social networks such as Facebook have many of these kinds of groups. You can join a general group covering all ex-pats in Uruguay, or go for something more specific such as a group for your hobby. These groups are great for asking for advice and making contacts.

goo.gl/FhrdYO

Leisure

There are loads of opportunities for leisure including numerous **public squares**, and **beaches** if you live near a large body of water. During daylight hours, public squares will always have people, but are rarely crowded. The beach and the **boardwalk** (*rambla*) are also great places to relax for free.

If you want to do some activity without joining a class the best option is to join a **public sports centre**. These centres offer the use of basketball courts and football pitches for free, along with classes such as cross fit for low prices (about $250 – USD 8.50). Each of these centres will have their own pricing system, but the maximum you should expect to pay is $500/month (USD 16.50), including the use of the swimming pool (provided they have one). To join you just need to bring 2 passport photos, a copy of your health card (*Carné de Salud*) and a $100 (USD 3.30) sign-up fee. After that you just pay for whatever additional activities you would like. For more information on where to find one of these, check the link below.

goo.gl/6uHBiV

SOCIAL and SPORTS CLUBS

Although public sports centres are popular, most locals prefer to pay for a social and sports club which specialised in whatever sport they have an interest. Montevideo has the highest density of these clubs, but they're pretty common in countryside town too.

goo.gl/xdXeeq

GYMS

Gyms are very popular in Uruguay, to the extent that you will find at least 2 of them in most neighbourhoods in Montevideo. The countryside has fewer options, but big towns and cities should have at least one good option. Most gyms in Uruguay keep up to date with current fitness trends, so you shouldn't have problem finding something that you like. To find a gym near you have a look at the websites linked below.

goo.gl/GM1zcK   **www.sinrutina.uy**

Clubs and Societies

In this section we have compiled a list of the websites of different clubs and associations around Uruguay. We suggest emailing the group you are interested in to find out prices, times and location but don't forget that most of the people will only speak Spanish. Often groups will give a test class for free, so that you can make sure the class is really for you.

While going through these listings, keep in mind that unless specifically indicated, all of these websites are going to be Spanish.

To help you along here is some important vocabulary:

Schedule – *Horarios*   **Location** – *Ubicación/Dirección*
Fees – *Tarifas/Precios*   **Contact** – *Contacto*

A

Acting
goo.gl/jeoZga
www.emad.edu.uy
goo.gl/eRCAyr

American Football
www.lufa.com.uy

Archery
www.cuarq.org
goo.gl/dKXWxl

Art
www.enba.edu.uy

Art of Living
www.elartedevivir.org.uy EN

Astronomy
www.aaa.org.uy
www.astronomia.edu.uy/sua

Athletics
www.atlecau.org.uy

Aviation
aauruguay.edu.uy
www.aerotecno.com EN
goo.gl/9qUwjP
www.aerosur.com.uy
www.puntaflightschool.com

B

Badminton
Asociación Uruguaya de Badminton
enrique@collerati.com
collerat@montevideo.com.uy

Basketball
www.fubb.org.uy

Basque Pelota
Marcello Filipeli
fup@adinet.com.uy

Billiards
www.febiu.com
billaruruguay.blogspot.com

Bird Watching
www.avesuruguay.org.uy
goo.gl/b3Mmnq

Bocce
goo.gl/P2VKyg
Sergio Malacrida
fubochas@gmail.com

Body Building
www.webaffu.org

Bowling
goo.gl/utsHOl
William Rodríguez
asoc.bowling.uy@gmail.com

Boxing
www.boxeouruguayo.com
goo.gl/GWH2vT

C

Candombe
goo.gl/waOf1o

Chess
www.fuajedrez.com

Collectibles
goo.gl/HDZ4Mk
www.monedasuruguay.com
www.megahobbyuruguay.com

Comics
goo.gl/8sif2T

Culinary
www.gatodumas.com.uy
www.bmarino.com.uy

-Bartending
www.audeb.com

-Children's Cooking
www.petitgourmet.edu.uy

Crafts
goo.gl/w2bW14
www.artesanos.uy
goo.gl/yys3Xt

Cricket
www.mvcc.com.uy EN

CrossFit / Calisthenics
www.calistenia.uy
www.instintocrossfit.com
www.crossfitcimarron.uy
www.crossfitmud.com
www.vaimacacrossfit.com
www.pandoraboxcrossfit.com
goo.gl/iJHmDe

Cycling
goo.gl/haqEyY

D

Dance
goo.gl/UmFOak
goo.gl/5E4nzq

-Aerial / Pole Dance
www.uruguaypoledance.com
www.poledanceuruguay.com.uy
www.mypole.uy

-Ballet
www.escueladeballet.com
www.balletcarrasco.com
www.inescamou.com

-Ballroom
www.facebook.com/EBDSD

-Belly Dance
goo.gl/W8hRGl

-Flamenco
goo.gl/Zbx2zC
goo.gl/GEyUV6

-Hip Hop
goo.gl/plW69t

-Salsa / Bachata
www.salsacompany.com.uy

-Tango / Milonga
goo.gl/B1Eyu9 EN
www.joventango.com
www.trasnochando.com.uy

Dog Training
goo.gl/rgJZwe
goo.gl/I7ptJN
www.escuelacolmillos.com

Drawing
juanjosemontans.com

E

Equestrian
goo.gl/Usqkjh
www.fude.org.uy

Extreme Sports
www.parkour.com.uy
goo.gl/bl84lk

F

Fencing
goo.gl/KHFqmW

Figure Skating
www.fudepyh.com

Film School
www.ecu.edu.uy
wp.uruguaycampusfilm.edu.uy
www.dodeca.org

Fishing
fupauruguay.com

Freemasonry
www.masoneriadeluruguay.org
www.granlogiafemuy.org
www.gofmu.org

Football
www.auf.org.uy
www.ligamud.com
www.ofi.org.uy
www.ligauniversitaria.org.uy
www.onfi.org.uy
www.fudefs.com
goo.gl/pkAtRJ
www.ligaempresarial.uy

-Football 5 pitch rental
goo.gl/zS5dUQ
goo.gl/esBoZy

-Football Referees
www.audaf.com.uy

G

Gaming
www.uga.com.uy

Gardening
www.jardinenuruguay.com
www.uruguaypaisajismo.com

Genealogy
www.iegu.org.uy

Go
goo.gl/WFAias

Golf
goo.gl/OlH5yz

Gymnastics
goo.gl/JPM091
Myriam Ordoñez
ejecutivofug2012@hotmail.com
ejecutivofug@hotmail.com

H

Handball
www.handballuruguay.com.uy

Hang Gliding
www.arribauruguay.com

Hash House Harriers
goo.gl/1UsqG9

Hiking
goo.gl/jTvyK1
goo.gl/tfp8iv

Hockey
www.hockey.com.uy
www.fudepyh.com

J

Judo
goo.gl/KvUQsC

K

Karate
www.ifk-uruguay.com

M

Make-Up Artist
www.elenazunino.com.uy
www.beautycenter.com.uy

Martial Arts
www.yamato.com.uy
goo.gl/OHTNlT

-Aikido
goo.gl/YbKuE7
www.aikido.com.uy

-Capoeira
goo.gl/SYubxS
goo.gl/Gx3Z4y

-Kung Fu
goo.gl/bLpgFo
goo.gl/zKW1Sr
www.wingchun.com.uy

-Tai Chi
www.taichi.com.uy

Mensa
goo.gl/Gb76Sq

MMA / Brazilian Jiu Jitsu / Kickboxing / Muay Thai
goo.gl/f24fOd
www.escorpion.com.uy
goo.gl/KhJuJa
goo.gl/NJmzmx
goo.gl/5Xnfds
www.jiujitsudaito.com
goo.gl/Xzhwyp
goo.gl/ePGhzg

Modeling
www.estilourbanomodels.com
www.modelosuy.com

Mountain Biking
www.mtb.uy

Murga
goo.gl/gCalVC
goo.gl/lTKP4F

Music
www.eumus.edu.uy
goo.gl/G5RkFk

O

Orienteering
goo.gl/XRwrkl

P

Padel
www.padel.com.uy

Paintball
www.paintballenuruguay.com

Paragliding
www.avolaruruguay.com

Pentathlon
Alcides Rodríguez
fedurupentatlon@gmail.com

Photography
www.fotoclub.org.uy
www.enba.edu.uy
www.tris.edu.uy

Poker
goo.gl/mC9S8s

Polo
goo.gl/4fwsC1
goo.gl/C1hfwC EN/PT
www.cpc.com.uy

Pottery
www.ceramicadelpez.edu.uy
www.tallerdart.com.uy

R

Reiki / Alternative Therapies
goo.gl/xMhx2w
www.anthu.org.uy

Rock Climbing
www.lamuralla.com.uy EN
goo.gl/JbSX7m

Roller Derby
goo.gl/6dBWs5

Roller Skating
www.fudepyh.com

Rowing
goo.gl/RU277X

Rugby
www.uru.org.uy EN

Running
www.atletas.com.uy

S

Sailing
www.ycu.org.uy
www.fuyv.org

Scrabble
www.scrabbel.org.uy

Sewing
www.eltallerdetere.com
www.cafecostura.com.uy

Shooting
www.cluburuguayodetiro.com
www.escueladetiro.com

Singing
goo.gl/X4aFjD
www.vocalcoach.com.uy
goo.gl/nHEzHd
goo.gl/PTwdWY

Skiing and Snowboarding
goo.gl/aWTAw1

Softball
Aldo Comastri
softballuy@adinet.com.uy

Sommelier
www.sommelieruruguay.com

Squash
www.uruguaysquash.com
www.boosturu.com
www.obcyogc.com

Swimming / Synchronized Swimming / Waterpolo
www.fun.org.uy

T

Table Tennis
www.futm.org

Taekwondo
www.taekwondouruguay.uy

Tandem Skydiving
goo.gl/tPbQS6
goo.gl/eCEgcE
goo.gl/fgD7bx

Tennis
www.aut.uy

Triathlon
www.triatlonuruguay.org

V

Volleyball
www.uruvoley.org.uy

Volunteer Work
goo.gl/FQxFVM
DE/PT/FR/IT/NL/ZH
www.techo.org/paises/uruguay

W

Water sports

-Diving
www.scubadiversuruguay.com
www.montevideodiving.com
www.yobuceo.com
www.octopus.com.uy

-Kayaking
goo.gl/nx721N
www.clubacal.org.uy
goo.gl/QfgSjU
Sebastián Gómez
fedurucanotaje@gmaill.com

-Kite / Windsurfing
www.facebook.com/AUWKS
www.kiteywindsurflaura.com
www.kitesurfuruguay.com
www.kitesurf.com.uy
www.windsurf.com.uy
www.oceanmind.net

-Stand Up Paddle Boarding
goo.gl/pWewGV

-Surfing
goo.gl/b7A1Vx
goo.gl/ijxg85
www.escuelasurflaolla.com
www.bajamar.com.uy
goo.gl/RjCvuE

-Wakeboarding
goo.gl/FnyA67

Weightlifting
goo.gl/bhVzqf

Whale Watching
goo.gl/5RlU1N

Wrestling
Dante Steffano
uru@fila-wrestling.com.uy

Y

Yoga
goo.gl/Msfexg
goo.gl/oxLu3L
www.sivananda.org.uy
www.satyananda.org.uy
www.kundaliniyogauruguay.com
www.theshackyoga.com **EN**

Z

Zumba
goo.gl/uZeswg

GETTING AROUND

In Uruguay the choice of transport is fairly limited, with buses cars and taxis being the only real options. In Montevideo publi transport covers most of the city, so you can get aroun comfortably without a car; however if you go to anothe department, you will need to think about getting some kind o private transport as bus coverage is very limited.

Buses

In general, city buses are crowded and uncomfortable, particularly during peak hours. Quality and prices vary greatly between departments and cities, as bus services are run by different companies.

COLONIA

In Colonia, buses are few and far between. Buses run rough every hour and a half, and service major towns. For mo information, check the link below.

www.omnibuscolonia.com.uy

MALDONADO

The bus services in Maldonado will bring you to the main are in the department, but is by no means comprehensive. Buses a fairly regular, and most will leave every 15 minutes during pe times. However you could be waiting for as long as an ho during off-peak periods.
To find out more, check the link below.

www.codesa.com.uy

MONTEVIDEO

The most comprehensive bus network is in Montevideo. Fares are uniform across the city, but increase regularly due to inflation. For information on the current price check the website below.

goo.gl/YNeDTl

To find out bus schedules check the website of the *Intendencia Municipal de Montevideo*. Keep in mind though, that because buses don't really stick to the schedule, it's a good idea to arrive at the bus stop 10 minutes before the bus is due to ensure you catch it.

www.montevideo.gub.uy/horariosSTM

To stop a bus, remember that you need to stick your arm out to flag it down. However, sometimes if the buses are full they'll just drive past and you'll have to wait for the next one. This may also happen if you have two buses driving directly behind each other. If you want to catch the second bus, you need to flag it with your arm high in the air or it won't stop.

STM Cards

These cards only apply to people living in Montevideo. They act as both as pre-paid and post-paid cards for your bus fare and are necessary to get hourly tickets.

For example, if you need to take two buses to get to your destination you can ask for a 1 hour ticket and pay the same price as you would for a single journey. This 1 hour ticket entitles you to take up to two buses within the hour. All you need to say is *"una hora"* when you are buying your ticket, and the ticket seller will show you where to put your card.

Similarly a 2 hour ticket (*dos horas*) will entitle you to take as many buses as you need within two hours. The price of this is cheaper than getting multiple single tickets, but more expensive than the 1 hour option.

Remember you must use your STM card for hourly tickets, ever if you do not have any money on it. Just hand the ticket selle cash after they scan your card.

These cards are available from special shops around the city an are free for first time users. Just make sure to bring an ID car when you are picking yours up. If you lose the card, you need t pay a replacement fee to the value of 2 single journeys.

For more information about the STM system check the website linked below.

goo.gl/9yNSwq

To locate a shop near you have a look here:

goo.gl/NPOQWq

Intercity Buses

If you want to move around the country using public transpor your only option is by bus. The main bus station in Uruguay **Tres Cruces**, which connects Montevideo to all of the other par of the country. This station also deals with international servic To find timetables and prices, just go to the *Horarios y Destin* section of the website linked below. Tickets for all companies a available at counters in the station, so there's no real need book online.

www.trescruces.com.uy

Although each major town and city has its own bus station, cities in the rest of the country aren't so well interconnected, so you may have a hard time getting to where you want to go without going through Montevideo. To find the best route we recommend going down to your local bus station and seeing what's on offer.

Taxis and Taxis Alternatives

Taxis are white with yellow roofs, and are pretty common in big cities. Fares vary depending on when you are travelling. If you are travelling at night in Montevideo between the hours of 22.00 and 6.00 the fares will be 20% higher than during daytime hours. Weekends and bank holidays will also have the night time rate, so it'll be a little more expensive to travel.

Taxis are all metered, but will show you a number representing distance rather than the price. The numbers always start at zero. All taxis have the price for each number written on a card in the back of the cab, so it's easy to keep track of your fare. Remember that the number zero represents the base fee, so you'll need to pay a small amount just for getting into the taxi. If you know where you're going it's a good idea to tell the driver which way you want to go, or you may find yourself taking the scenic route.

As being a taxi driver can be a dangerous job, the front and the back of taxis are divided by a plastic screen to ensure the drivers safety.

Uber has also recently set up shop in Montevideo, providing a competitive and more comfortable alternative to traditional taxis. To find an app for a taxi or an Uber have a look in our Apps section.

Trains

Trains in Uruguay are rare, to the extent that most people don't even know that there are any. However, they do exist, and serve some parts of Montevideo and Canelones.

To find information on the different stops and tariffs, check the website below. It's one of the few available in English!

www.afe.com.uy EN

International Ferries Companies

If you want to visit Buenos Aires, you can travel by ferry fr Montevideo and Colonia. The journey is pretty short, though c be on the expensive side. For more information, check the lir below.

www.buquebus.com EN/DE/PT   **www.coloniaexpress.com**
www.cacciolaviajes.com   **www.seacatcolonia.com** EN

Bikes

Cycling is a common method of transport. Just remember it is not safe to leave your bike on the street, even with a lock, as it will get stolen.

Since 2015 a public bicycle rental scheme called **Movete** has been operating in Montevideo. This includes 80 bikes, with 8 different stations, however all of them are located in Ciudad Vieja.

If you want to subscribe, bring your **STM card** to a help centre and they will set you up. If you don't have a card they will issue one there, so don't worry. You can find more information about it on the following link.

movete.montevideo.gub.uy

Personal Vehicles

Cars are the most common form of private transport in Uruguay, though motorbikes come in at a close second. Although

Montevideo is congested most of the time, traffic in the rest of the country is normally free-flowing.

Be aware that in Montevideo refuse collectors use horse and carts to get around the city, so watch out for these on the road.

CARS and MOTORCYCLES

Having a car or a motorcycle is a must for many, as publi transport can be slow and inefficient. However, many expats fin that using Uruguayan roads can be quite stressful as traffi lights and road markings seem to be more like suggestions rathe than rules.
It is also worth noting that Uruguayans drive on the right han side of the road, which can be a big adjustment for people comin from countries where they drive on the left.

The price of gas is also amongst the highest in the world, an can increase up to twice a year due to inflation.
To get an idea of how much it costs at the moment, check the lin below.

www.unvenu.org.uy

DRIVER'S LICENSE

Getting a Uruguayan driver's license should be relative straight forward. If you have a valid foreign license you have period of grace of six months before you need to convert it to Uruguayan one. To do this you will need to go to the City Hc (*Intendencia*). Queues can be long, so if it's possible try a make an appointment.

You will need to bring your ID card (*Cédula*), your driver's licen your passport with a stamp showing that you entered the count less than a year ago, a health certificate from an approved clir (*Carné de Salud*), a translation of your licence if it isn't writt in the Latin alphabet (e.g. if it's in Japanese or Arabic), and t fee (this will vary between departments).
The easiest place to do this is in **Montevideo**. For mc information about the procedure there, follow the link below:

goo.gl/l12IzX

If you live in **Canelones**, the process will be a little more complicated, as they will also ask you for a **consular certificate proving the authenticity of your license**. This should include the details of types of vehicles you will be driving, the passengers you will carry, and the payload capacity of the car you will be using. If this document is not in Spanish, it will need to be translated by a certified translator. This will be required in addition to all of the other documents listed above. You may also be asked to take a theory and a practical driving test on the day.

To avoid doing this, we recommend making a trip to Montevideo, but if you really want to do it in Canelones, check the link below for more information.

goo.gl/js9zli

If you're getting your **license for the first time** you should check the link below for everything you'll need. It has links to the theory test manual, along with accredited driving schools, and details about fees.

goo.gl/hBtJ1u

BUYING A CAR

Buying a car is a relatively simple process. Both new and second hand cars are in plentiful supply, both in standard dealerships, and through other sources.

Below we have compiled a list of links for the not so standard places to get a car.

goo.gl/hYPsfM	**goo.gl/OS6sPN**
www.oautos.com.uy	**goo.gl/NQZ2FC**

Once you have chosen your car you will need to hire a notary (*escribano*) to help you begin the purchasing process. They will handle everything, from checking that the car has not been stolen, to registering it in the appropriate department, and transferring the title.

To find a notary, check the link below.

www.aeu.org.uy

RENTAL CARS

Renting a car is a great option for those who can't afford the everyday costs of a car, but who want the freedom of driving for a weekend. Uruguay has many car rental services for cars of all different sizes and price ranges. Search through the websites below to find what suits you or for different price quotes. Remember that prices can change depending on the season.

www.avis.com.uy EN/PT   **www.multicar.com.uy** EN

www.budget.com.uy EN/PT   **hertz.com.uy** EN/PT

www.europcar.com.uy EN/PT   **www.puntacar.com.uy** EN

PARKING

Parking on the street is common all around the country, though you will also find some car parks in some buildings and shopping centres. These are generally used by people who want to keep the car safe at night.

For the most part, people leave their cars on the street during the day, though be aware that you will need to pay a fee in some areas.

In Montevideo the price of a ticket is $35 for an hour (as of January 2017). Tickets can be purchased in shops such as **Abitab** or **Redpagos**, or by **SMS**.

If you want to pay by **SMS**, send a message to **466**, with "E" your license plate and the number of minutes you want to pay for (in blocks of 30 or 60 minutes).

For example: **E STU1234 60**

STU1234 is the license plate number and 60 is the number of minutes you want to pay for.

As you are leaving your parking spot, you may also notice a person helping you to reverse out. This person is not doing this for the good of their health, and is expecting to be tipped (normally $5 should suffice).

TOLLS

Toll roads are fairly common in Uruguay, particularly between departments. On the website below you can find the current toll rates, along with information on buying a **Telepeaje stick**, which will allow you to pay later **by card**, rather than fumbling for change at the toll booth.

goo.gl/9pXN2t

INSURANCE

All vehicles need to have basic insurance (SOA) that covers personal damage to a third person.

For more information, have a look at the following link:

goo.gl/bfNwps

If you want more comprehensive insurance you can contact some of the following companies, or alternatively find an insurance broker to get you a quote from several different companies.

Major Car Insurance Companies

www.bse.com.uy
www.segurossura.com.uy
www.portoseguro.com.uy

Insurance Broker's Association

www.aproase.com.uy

Uruguay may not suit people with disabilities, particularly i
they have mobility issues. Broken footpaths, no pedestria
crossings and inaccessible public transport can make it ver
difficult to move around. In addition, although Uruguay ha
equal opportunities legislation, finding a job can still be difficul

In the section below we'll give an overview of the service
available, though you can also use the following links to fin
more specific information about associations, activities
entitlements and subsidies for people with disabilities i
Uruguay.

pronadis.mides.gub.uy   **discapacidad.gub.uy**

Wheelchair Access

Uruguay is not a wheelchair
friendly country. Broken footpaths
make moving around for anyone
difficult and much of the public
transport is not equipped to deal
with wheelchairs. Wheelchair
ramps are also few and far between
so moving from footpaths to roads is
difficult. This also applies to getting into
certain buildings.

If you don't want to use public transport, **taxis are cheap a**
plentiful, though most aren't set up to cater for wheelchai
Most will have space in the back, so you'll need to make su
your wheelchair is collapsible. Alternatively you can book a se
with **CNHD**, whose vehicles have all been specially adapted f
people with reduced mobility. This is a door to door servi
though it is shared with other users so it requires time flexibili

goo.gl/f5Aaox

If you are looking for a nice day out, take a look at the *Parque de la Amistad*. It is located in Montevideo and is the first fully-accessible public space in Uruguay.

goo.gl/1knq1L

Services for the Blind and Visually Impaired

The Uruguayan National Union for the Blind provides many services, from Braille lessons and mobility training, to theatre. They also work with job placement and inclusion in education. For more information, check the link below.

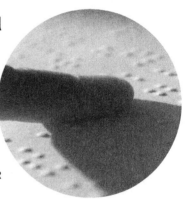

www.uncu.org.uy

If you are interested in **drama**, you can also have a look at *Teatro Ciego Uruguay*.

goo.gl/ltkNNO

If you need a **guide dog** contact Federation for Guide Dogs in Uruguay (Fundappas). They provide free guide dogs for the right candidates and also accept volunteers to help train new dogs.

fundappas-uruguay.org

The Deaf Community

The main challenge deaf people will probably encounter in Uruguay is the language barrier. If you can't communicate effectively in Spanish or if you do not know Uruguayan sign language, making yourself understood will be difficult. This difficulty will be intensified by the severe shortage of sign language interpreters which will make performing many official tasks tricky to say the least.

If you need a **sign language interpreter**, the Association o Uruguayan Sign Language Interpreters (*Asociación de Intérprete de Lengua de Señas Uruguaya*) will be able to help you. You ca get in contact by email at **ailsu2008@hotmail.com**

For more information on activities or services run by the Dea community we recommend contacting the **Uruguaya Association for the Deaf**, linked below.

goo.gl/wuIuFD   **goo.gl/DSK1dz**

The Association for Parents and Friends of the Deaf is also great website to find out more information about the Dec community in Uruguay.

www.apasu.org.uy

If you wish to enroll your child in a school that caters for th deaf, have a look at the following website. In general educatic is mixed, with some schools providing separate classes for th deaf, and others providing an interpreter. All of these schoo are located in Montevideo.

www.cereso.org

If you are interested in learning **sign language** follow the link below to find different courses around Montevideo and Maldonado.

www.cinde.net

UNEXPECTED COSTS

While in Uruguay you shouldn't be taken by surprise by unexpected costs, though to avoid any misunderstandings, we've gone into detail on some you do need to look out for.

Tips

Tipping is common in **restaurants** and **taxis**, with the standard practice being to round up what you have paid to the nearest note. For example, if you pay $475 for your meal, you should round up to $500, leaving $25 as a tip. Alternatively, if you are in a taxi and your bill is $74 you should round it up to $80. If you do not want to round up in a restaurant, leaving 10% of the total cost is also acceptable.

It's also customary to tip $5 - $10 to **delivery guys** and **petrol pump attendants** (*pisteros*). *Pisteros* will also normally provide you with the additional services of cleaning your windscreen along with checking the oil level and the air pressure in your tyres.

You may also come across windscreen cleaners or street artists at traffic lights in major junctions. If you want your windscreen cleaned tip $2 - $4, and if you don't want it cleaned, just catch their eye, shake your head and look straight ahead. Some may clean your window anyway, but in that case you can just drive on without tipping.

n a Restaurant

he biggest hidden costs you will come across will be in estaurants. Often if there is a **breadbasket** on the table, it will mean extra money. Some restaurants will charge for bread eaten, and others will charge simply for the basket being out.

Another unexpected charge is the **seating charge** (*cubierto*), which refers to the charge you need to pay for using the cutlery (though you can't bring your own!). Similarly, an **artistic charge** (*cubierto artístico*) may also apply if there is a live show on that night. Some restaurants will tell you about this charge in advance, bu in others, it's best to ask.

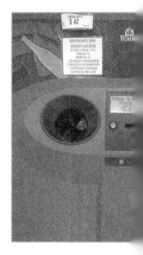

Returnable Bottles

If you ever buy bottles of either beer or soft drinks, you'll probably notice that it costs a little more than expected. This is because you have to **pay a deposit** on the bottle, which is refunded once you return it. This is charged on 1 litre glass bottles for certain brands of beer and soft drinks, and also on 1.5 litre soft drink bottles made out of hard plastic. Some wine bottles may also require a deposit, but it's uncommon. This additional cost will not be included in the marked price.

Most supermarkets will have an area dedicated to the return these bottles. They issue a receipt to the value of the bottl returned, which you can then reclaim when you are purchasi something in-store. Many corner shops also accept return bottles, so long as they stock the same brand of beer as t bottle you are returning. If you are returning bottles to a corn shop, you normally just need to show the clerk the bottles, a they'll deduct the value from the cost of your purchases.

HELPFUL MOBILE APPS

Uruguay is not a particularly tech crazy country, though more and more apps are being developed locally to make life easier. Here you will find the ones we thought were especially useful, divided into those that are only applicable to Montevideo, and those that are applicable to the whole country.

Nationwide Apps

Paganza
Paying your bills

Mercado Libre
Buy and sell

PedidosYa
Food delivery

Easy
Taxi finder

Uruguay Presente
Taxi alternative

Montevideo Apps

STM Montevideo
Bus journey planner

SoloBus Montevideo
Bus journey planner

Voy en Taxi
Taxi finder

Uber
Taxi alternative

Montevideo Parkin
On-street parking

Remember that if you are using your phone in public, to pay clos‹ attention to your surroundings, as phone theft is pretty common.

LOCAL LANGUAGE

Spanish is the official language in Uruguay, and the only one that's widely spoken. You will find people who speak other languages, such as English and Portuguese, or if you live near Brazil, Portuñol. These are however the exception and not the norm. With this in mind, we recommend having at least a basic level of Spanish before you arrive.

If you already speak Spanish, the key thing to take note of is that Uruguay has its own unique dialect of Spanish, different from Spain and other Latin-American countries. For example the *"ll"* and the *"y"* sounds are more similar to the *"sh"* sound in English.

If you speak Spanish from Spain you will also need to readjust some of your vocabulary, for example the word *"coger"* (to take) in Spain means something very different in Uruguay. You should say *"agarrar"* instead. Similarly the word *"vos"* is used instead of *"tú"* to say *"you"*.

Spanish Words and Phrases

If you didn't get a chance to learn any Spanish, here are some basic phrases to get you started.

> **Hello** – Hola - *ola*
> **Good morning** - Buen día - *bwen dee-a*
> **How are you?** - ¿Cómo andás? - *komo an-dass?*
> **Fine** - Bien - *bee-en*
> **Please** - Por favor - *por fa-vor*
> **Thank you** – Gracias – *gra-see-ass*

Language Schools

If you want to continue learning Spanish after you arrive, taking lessons is a good idea, particularly if you have a low level of

Spanish. **La Herradura** is an immersion school, who combine
Spanish lessons with social activities, internships and volunteer
work. This can be a great way to give your Spanish a kick-start.
They have a branch in both Montevideo and Punta del Este.

www.spanish-herradura.com EN/DE/PT

Below is a list with other language schools in Uruguay. Most
offer intensive courses, and are aimed at people coming to
Uruguay for the purpose of studying Spanish and also offer
homestays and cultural activities as part of the price. If you
don't have time for an intensive course, or if you're just looking
to brush up a little, some schools also offer conversational
classes and less intensive courses.

www.academiauruguay.com EN/PT/DE/FR
www.spanishuruguay.com EN/PT/IT/RU
www.voshablas.com.uy EN/DE/FR
shadi-enbashi.squarespace.com EN/DE
studyabroadcourses.com EN
www.casadobrasil.com.uy

If you plan on living somewhere and integrating fully into the society it is a good idea to try and learn something about the political and social affairs that affect your new home. This can be easily done by browsing through a newspaper or watching the news.

In Uruguay there are no dedicated English language newspapers, but the **South Atlantic News Agency** will cover some of the news in Uruguay as well as news from the surrounding region.

en.mercopress.com/uruguay

If you have a good grasp of Spanish, **El Observador** and **El País** are great options to keep on top of current events. Both are free and will give you a good idea of current affairs in Uruguay.

www.elobservador.com.uy

www.elpais.com.uy

CUSTOMS TO GET USED TO

As in any country, Uruguay has many different customs to ge
used to if you are going to settle in.
Being able to adjust to these can mean the difference betwee
leaving after a year and staying forever.

Greeting People

People greet each other by **kissing once on the right cheek**. Thi
includes women to women and men to women. For men greetin
other men they have never met before a handshake is expecter
though if do they know each other, a kiss is fine.

Uruguayans greet each other with a kiss every time they see eac
other and every time they say goodbye. It's common to see sho
assistants kissing each other as they come into work, even if the
are in the middle of a transaction.

If you are socialising it is very important to kiss everyone in tl
group, or you may end up offending someone.

Eating and Drinking

MEALTIMES

In Uruguay dinner is normally eaten between 8pm and 11pm.
fill in the gap between lunch and dinner, most **Uruguayans e
an extra meal called *merienda***. This is usually eaten wheneu
you arrive home from work or school, which is normally betwe
5pm and 7pm. It often consists of crackers, *bizcochos* (savou
pastries from the local bakery), bread with butter or *dulce
leche* and *café con leche* (hot milk with coffee) or *mate*.

On the 29th of the month it is also customary to eat gnocc
Before you begin eating you should put money under your pl
to attract good fortune.

ASADO

Asado is the kind of BBQ eaten in Uruguay. It's made on a wood burning grill called a *parrilla* and is very personal for each family. During the summer having an *asado* is one of the most common ways to spend an evening. It's also eaten in winter, though normally only on the weekends as it doubles as a social activity.

If you are invited to one of these in the evening time, be aware that you normally won't start eating until around 11pm. There will usually be snacks to tide you over, but nevertheless, we wouldn't recommend going too hungry.

It's also important to remember that while you may want to help the host, **touching any equipment used to make the meat is considered rude**, unless you are invited to do so.

MATE

Mate is a bitter green tea made out of *yerba mate*. It is drunk out of a wooden gourd called a *mate* or *calabaza* using a metal straw called a *bombilla*. You will see it everywhere you go. People drink it while doing the shopping, at work or even while skateboarding. It is also often passed around a circle of friends and family while catching up on the day's events.

Mate is a deeply personal thing for each Uruguayan. Each person has their own preference for the kind of *yerba* they like to drink, how hot they like the water, and how big they like the *mate* gourd to be.

If you would like to have your own *mate*, we recommend going to the market with a Uruguayan to explain the different choices to you. Remember that before you can drink out of the gourd you must first cure it using old *yerba* or else the inside will crack.

To drink *mate* like a Uruguayan, you should also get a thermos. *Mate* is meant to be drunk over a long period of time, so a thermos is essential for keeping the water at the correct temperature.

Politics, Football and Religion

Politics, football and religion are the three subjects best avoid
if you don't want to start an argument. Most Uruguayans w
have strong opinions on each of these topics and will not
afraid to share them. Friendships have been lost over less,
discuss them at your own risk.

Football

Football is the be all and end all in Uruguay. It is so importa
that it affects the mood of the entire country. When Urugu
wins, it feels as though the whole nation has won the lotte
and when they lose, it's as though a cloud of depression h
descended.

Unfortunately passion for football can sometimes turn i
violence, so be careful on the streets on Derby Day!

Breaking the Rules

Many Uruguayans live by a philosophy called *viveza criolla*, which literally translates to "native cunning". This means breaking small rules in the day to day, or taking advantage of mistakes or inattention. Examples of this include underpaying at restaurants, or not letting someone know if they've given you the wrong change. Some people will even go as far as "sharing" someone else's TV connection or electricity supply. It's commonly believed that if there's a law, there's a loophole.

While this shouldn't affect your day to day life too much, you may sometimes find yourself left with the sensation that you're not getting the full picture.

Using the Bathroom

A common feature in toilets is the bidet. As exciting as this may seem we would not recommend using them if it is not in your own home, as they may not be as clean as you might hope.

Money for Judas

From the middle of November up to the 24th of December, groups of children make a puppet out of old clothes and fill it up with old newspapers. After this they set up shop with the puppet on the streets of their neighbourhood and ask for a coin for Judas (*Una monedita pa'l Juda*). With this money they'll buy fireworks, to be shoved inside the Judas at midnight on the 24th and ignited.

The Last Cyclist

Uruguayans often say that the year doesn't really start until after the last cyclist of the *Vuelta Ciclista* arrives. This 75 year old cycling competition is held during Easter week, and the end of it signifies that the real work of the year has begun. Before this most Uruguayans like to take things easy and enjoy the fine weather. Very often the last cyclist of the race gets as much coverage as the winner.

On the Beach

One of the more unusual Uruguayan customs, happens durir
sunset on the beach. Many Uruguayans gather in the evening
watch the sun set, clapping as it disappears behind the horizo
This is to thank the sun for a beautiful day.

Another time you may hear spontaneous clapping on the bea
is when a child gets lost. Uruguayans clap their hands if a lo
child has been found to let the parents know that their wander
has been found, so don't be too surprised when an applau
break out.

RELIGION

Uruguay is largely considered the most secular nation in South America. The Church-state split was established in the 1919 Constitution, resulting in absolute religious freedom.

Many Uruguayans do not actively practice any religion, with 23.5% of the population claiming to believe in God, but not religion and 17.2% identifying as agnostic.

The most prevalent religion is **Roman Catholicism**, with 47.1% of the population (many non-practicing), followed by **Protestantism** at 11.1% of the people. **Judaism** has a tiny community, with 0.4% of the population practicing, and **Islam** is practically non-existent, with only about 0.01% of people practicing.

There are also other African based religions such as **Macumba** and **Umbanda** practiced in Uruguay.

Roman Catholicism

As mentioned, Roman Catholicism is the biggest religion in Uruguay, though church attendance is quite low. To find a church near you check the link below. This website also provides a schedule for mass times for many of the churches.

goo.gl/itfalY

Remember that most masses will only be in Spanish, so if you want to be an active member of the community, it's important to start learning!

For news and updates on the Catholic Church in Uruguay, check the following link: **www.iglesiacatolica.org.uy**

Protestantism

There are many different active protestant religions in Uruguay, with the **Methodist Church** being the most popular. To find a Methodist Church near you check the link below. The website is entirely in Spanish, but Church listings can be found easily enough in the "*Directorio*" section.

www.imu.org.uy

The **Anglican Church** is also active in Uruguay. To find one i your area have a look at the link below. You can find a churc or a mission by searching in the "*Parroquias y misiones*" sectio

www.uruguay.fedigitales.org

Judaism

The Jewish community in Uruguay is tiny. Most of the synagogu are centred in **Montevideo** and **Punta del Este**, though there also a small community in **Paysandú**. Outside of these are kosher food is almost unheard of, so you might want to take th into consideration if you plan on keeping kosher.

To find a synagogue in Montevideo check the link to the directory below.

goo.gl/1fRdsQ

If you plan on keeping kosher the following blog has loads of good tips and recommendations for restaurants in Montevideo.

goo.gl/Wn9xb1

To find a synagogue and kosher shops and restaurants in Punta del Este follow the link below. *"Sinagogas"* is where you'll find links to Synagogues and *"Servicios de comida"* is where you'll find the addresses of kosher shops and restaurants.

goo.gl/jfSe6z

To find out more information about Jewish life in Uruguay check the two links below.

www.cciu.org.uy   **www.jai.com.uy**

Islam

The Islamic community in Uruguay is tiny, with practitioners numbering in the hundreds. There are no mosques and finding halal food can be very difficult. There are however 4 prayer centres in Montevideo. For more information on them check the links below.

Islam Uruguay: **islamuruguay.com**
Islamic Center of Uruguay: **centroislamicouruguay.com.uy**
Centre of Egyptian Islamic Culture: **goo.gl/DzcVGL**

Umbanda

Umbanda is practiced by a small percentage of Uruguayans, with 0.6% of the population identifying it as their religion. It is a blend of African traditions, Catholicism and Indigenous American beliefs. Practitioners of Umbanda believe in a pantheon of gods and the spirit world.

The most famous deity in Uruguay is **Iemanja**, a goddess who lives in the sea. On February 2ⁿᵈ believers will flock to *Playa Ramírez* in Montevideo to perform rituals and offer gifts to her. Many non-believers will also go along to watch.

To learn more about this have a look at the website linked below

goo.gl/3BKPoC

Macumba

Macumba is a kind of Umbanda. Most Uruguayans associate with **black magic**, and many don't feel comfortable with it. Th most obvious sign of Macumba is a dead chicken, with corn an oranges left on a street corner. This is a common enough sight i Montevideo, so don't be surprised!

Cábala

In Uruguay *Cábala* refers to the good luck rituals people perfor to make sure they continue having luck. Each person's ritual personal and can include things like only entering a footbc pitch with the right foot, gambling in the same newsagent, matter where you are, or wearing lucky underwear.

This belief is deeply rooted in Uruguayan culture, and mo people will have a *Cábala* for different events in their lives e going for a job interview, watching a football match or going vote. Even if good luck is not brought by repeating the *Cába* most Uruguayans won't abandon their personal ritual as th belief in it is so strong.

FAMILY SERVICES

Moving to Uruguay with a family can be a tricky undertaking, particularly if you have kids of a school age. The ex-pat community is relatively small, so it can be difficult to find support from people in a similar situation to yourself. In this section we'll go through things like finding a school or a childminder, to try and make the process as painless as possible.

Schools

Public schools in Uruguay are all secular and free. Mandatory schooling starts from the age of 4, when your child should be enrolled in a **kindergarten**. This lasts for two years. The next stage is **primary school**, which is six years long and caters for children between the ages of 6 and 12. **Secondary school** takes another three years and is for teenagers between the ages of 12 and 15. After that you can choose to do a *Bachillerato*, but this is not mandatory. It takes three years and is the equivalent of finishing high school or secondary school. It also allows you to apply for a university.

During primary school, and the first cycle of secondary school, subjects are general, and aim to provide the student with a solid base of knowledge. The *Bachillerato* years are normally more specialised, and aim to provide a base for further study in university.

Uruguay is also committed to digital education and promoting the use of laptops in the classroom. To help this along, the government has given every student and teacher a special laptop as part of a project called **Plan Ceibal**.

For any questions you may have about any aspect of the school system, check the link below.

goo.gl/nzB9sR

Public vs Private School

Public education is of a good standard, though many Uruguayan try to send their children to private schools. This is not due to the quality of the education, but rather because private school offer extra services and curricula. Public education is also entirely through Spanish, with little focus on English, which why many expat parents prefer to send their children to private schools.

Most expat children attend **international schools**, as many them are bi-lingual and some parents prefer to choose a school with a curriculum from their home country. Below are links with information on different pre-schools, primary schools and secondary schools, mostly located near Montevideo. Please remember that all schools set their own entry requirements.

richardanderson.edu.uy EN
www.woodlands.edu.uy EN
www.uas.edu.uy EN
www.stellamaris.edu.uy EN
woodsideschool.edu.uy
www.stbrendan.edu.uy

www.dsm.edu.uy DE
www.lf.edu.uy FR
portal.british.edu.uy/web EN
www.escuelaintegral.edu.uy
www.scuolaitaliana.edu.uy
www.stpatrick.edu.uy

Entry Requirements for Secondary School

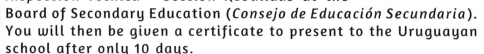

Entering the public school system is easy and free. You just need to submit your child's passport, ID card (*Cédula*), and a translated and legalised certificate of education from your home country to the *Inspección Técnica – Sección Reválidas* at the Board of Secondary Education (*Consejo de Educación Secundaria*). You will then be given a certificate to present to the Uruguayan school after only 10 days.

The deadline to apply for this is the 30th October for students in the junior cycle (years 1-3), and the 30th June for students in the senior cycle (years 4-6).

Entry Requirements for a Public University

Getting into a public university (*Universidad de la República*) is very difficult for foreign students as there are a lot of requirements that are difficult to adhere to. For example, you need to prove that you've been living in Uruguay for at least 3 years, and that you have moved there because a member of your nuclear family needed to, or that you have a family member in a diplomatic position. You also need a conversion certificate for your secondary school qualification. (See our chapter on Revaluing your Degree).

If you don't meet these requirements, going to a private university is your only option. These are much easier to get into, but cost money.

Childcare

Childcare is plentiful, but is offered mainly through Spanish. If you want some good recommendations, it's a good idea to ask around at your child's school.

Some schools also offer child minding services before and after school hours. This is called **doble horario** and is pretty common in private schools.

In the link below you will find a search engine for childcare centres in most departments in Uruguay.

goo.gl/KmDmjB

Family Activities

Family days are normally spent in public parks, or if the weather is nice, on the beach. There are not many child-centred indoor activities, though the cinema is always an option. Below we have listed two activities designed especially for children, located in Canelones and Montevideo.

The first is called *Fútbol Golf*. This is a golf green for both children and adults where the aim is to play a round of golf but through football.

www.futbolgolf-soca.com EN/DE

The second is an interactive museum dedicated to science and technology called *Espacio Ciencia*. The website for this available in English.

www.latu.org.uy/espaciociencia EN

PETS

Pets in Uruguay are really common. Most families have a dog, which means there are plenty of pet friendly open spaces, and cats are safe to wander in residential areas and in the countryside. In this section we'll go through all you need to know about having a pet in Uruguay.

Bringing your Pet

Bringing your cat or dog to Uruguay is not difficult, though it does require preparation. Healthy animals, with the correct documentation are not quarantined, so it's important to make sure you have all of the necessary paperwork to avoid unnecessary stress for your pet.

To bring your cat or dog to Uruguay, you will need the following documents:

➡ **A Veterinary Certificate.** This can be acquired from a licensed veterinarian, and must be issued within 10 days of departure. It should state that your pet is healthy, and free from parasites and communicable diseases.

The certificate should also state the country of origin of the animal, and the destination, along with the name and address of the owner, and details about the animal, such as: name, date of birth, sex, breed, size, coat, and distinguishing marks.

The forms should then be signed by the Minister for Agriculture in your country. If in doubt about who to ask, check with your vet, or your nearest Uruguayan Consulate.

➡ **A Rabies Certificate** should also be included with the Veterinary Certificate. This should show that your pet has had a rabies vaccination no sooner than 30 days, but no later than a year before coming to Uruguay. It should also contain the brand of vaccination used. This is only applicable to animals over 3 months old.

⇒ If you have a dog, it must be treated for the **Echinococcus tapeworm** no less than 72 hours, and no more than 30 days before arrival. The treatment must have **Praziquantel as an active ingredient**.

⇒ Please note that any animal that has been previously diagnosed with **Leishmaniasis** will not be let in to Uruguay.

Aside from cats and dogs, **animals are treated as an import**, so you will need to go through the importation process. For more information on that check our Restricted Items section.

For more information about any kind of pet, please check the website of Ministry for Livestock, Agriculture and Fisheries (*Ministerio de Ganadería, Agricultura y Pesca*) using the following link: **goo.gl/Hb3cua**

Alternatively you can also contact Dr. Rosario Guererro at the **Animal Health Division** (*División de Sanidad Animal*) in the Department for the Control of International Trade inside the Ministry for Livestock, Agriculture and Fisheries, using the following email address: **rguerrero@mgap.gub.uy**

Before you go it's also important to check your **airline's policy** on animals. Some will allow the animal in the cabin, and others only in the hold. For more information about different airlines or to find a pet friendly hotel, have a look at the link below.

www.pettravel.com EN

Adopting a Pet

If you live in a city, locating a pet shop nearby shouldn't be too difficult. Dogs and cats are the most common pets, but it's easy enough to find pets such as birds and rabbits too. If you want anything more exotic, you might have a problem.

If you want to adopt an **abandoned animal** *Animales Sin Hogar* is a great place to search. They have pictures of the animals on their website and also opportunities to volunteer.

www.animalessinhogar.com.uy

Dog Licenses (*Patente*)

Dogs need to have a license, and this needs to be renewed every year. They cost $530 (USD 18) and can be gotten from your vet's office. Once you have it, you should display it from your dog's collar. If your dog gets caught without a license you are liable to pay a fine of up to 10 times the amount of the cost of the license.

Veterinary Services

Veterinary services in Uruguay are of a very high standard, though many vets will not speak English. To find a vet in your area have a look at this link: **goo.gl/ohyeXQ**

Health concerns in Uruguay are relatively few. Tap water is safe to drink, and there are no vaccination requirements prior to entry.

The biggest health concern for most expats is the strength of the sun during the summer. Uruguay is directly affected by the **hole in the ozone layer** over the South Pole, which means that even people who are used to the heat will burn easily. To stay safe use sun cream with both UVA and UVB protection, and **check the UV index** before you go out. The link below will give you a hourly forecast of the UV index in your area and let you know what times of the day are the most dangerous to be out in.

sunburnmap.com EN/DE/FR/RU

The Health Care System

Health care in Uruguay is excellent, and also quite diverse. There are several different kinds of providers, all of which we'll detail below. The system is divided into private and public care, with the main difference between the two being the comfort level of the different medical centres.

PRIVATE HEALTH CARE

Private health care largely comprises of a kind of health care centre called a *"mutualista"* or a *"sociedad médica"*. These centres are like huge private clinics staffed by different types of doctors and are the most common place to go for routine check up for all kinds of ailments. They are different from hospitals in that hospitals normally deal more with emergency, or non routine procedures, such as a surgery, although if you do need surgery, this is also normally arranged through your doctor the *sociedad médica*.

Most *mutualistas* have one main centre and some may also have smaller poly-clinics. Each will also have an affiliated hospital.

If you want to become a member of a *sociedad médica*, simply go to the clinic and request a membership. Each has set requirements regarding age and pre-existing conditions, and each requires a medical exam to join.

Once you become a member, you will have to pay a set fee every month. If you are an employee, your employer will pay this as a part of the taxes on your salary, however once you have chosen your *mutualista*, you cannot change it for a year. Keep in mind that in some plans you may be required to pay an additional fee for each visit, but that will all be discussed when setting up your plan.

To find a *sociedad médica* in your area, have a look through the link below.

goo.gl/b9q78c

HOUSECALL SERVICES

Emergencias móviles is an on-call doctor service for house calls. People normally use this for small accidents or illnesses. It is especially popular amongst people with children. The service is very quick, and is great in cases where you need medical help immediately. They will also send an ambulance much quicker than a *mutualista* if you need to be transferred to a medical facility.

Fees for this are paid on a monthly basis, and different plans are available depending on your needs.

Below is a list of the most popular companies. Check each to see which suits you the best.

www.ucm.com.uy   www.semm.com.uy   www.suat.com.uy

PUBLIC HEALTH CARE

Public health care is available to everyone, but the level of comfort in the facilities is a little lower than in private establishments.

For a list of public hospitals follow the link below, choose "Centros Asistenciales" from the left-hand side of the page and select your region.

www.asse.com.uy

Dentists

Dentists in Uruguay are also top class, and not too expensive. Most practices are private, but some *sociedades médicas* will also cover dental costs.

To find a private dentist in your area, use the link below.

goo.gl/A8lNPf

Women's Health

Women are entitled to take a day off work for both a Pap smear and a mammogram. By law this should be a paid day off.

Pharmacies

Pharmacies are widespread and can be easily identified by the logo of a yellow cross inside a blue circle. Although they are usually small-time businesses, there are a few chains, with the biggest being **Farmashop**.

www.farmashop.com.uy

Pharmacies come well stocked with medication, but many do not have a lot of choice for cosmetic items. If you have any medical issues, remember that medication prescribed by a doctor comes with a discount in all pharmacies, and if you're looking for further savings, prescribed medication sold at health providers is even cheaper still.

Travel Insurance

Comprehensive insurance is very important when you are moving country. Most people will buy travel insurance before leaving their own country to insure against misadventures while flying and to cover the first few months abroad.

A good provider for countries all over the world is **HCCMIS**, which is linked below.

www.hccmis.com EN

Alternatively you can research companies in your own country to try and find the one with the best deal. Ideally your health insurance should cover air ambulances, hospital stays, and a member of your family flying over if you are in really bad shape.

EMERGENCY CONTACTS

The emergency number in Uruguay is not too difficult t◄ remember. In the case of a fire, a crime or a health emergenc◄ you can call **911**.

Here are some simple phrases to help you communicate in cas◄ of an emergency:

I need help - Necesito ayuda
neh–seh–see–toe a-shoe-dah

I got robbed – Me robaro
meh ro-ba-ro◄

I need a doctor – Necesito un doctor
neh–seh–see–toe oon dok-tor

I have an emergency – Tengo una emergencia
teng-o oo-na e-mer-khen-sya

There is a fire in my house – Hay un incendio en mi casa
I oon in-send-io en me kasa

We would also recommend that you keep the number of yo◄ country's embassy in Uruguay to hand in case you run into a◄ problems. You can find it using the following link: **goo.gl/I6ycF**

STAYING SAFE

Security in Uruguay is a big issue, but not as bad as in neighbouring Argentina and Brazil. To help you stay safe, we have put together some advice for avoiding troublesome situations.

At Home

Home security is really important as break-ins are not unheard of. Most homes will have gates around their property and bars on the windows, so you just need to make sure to lock up properly before you leave.

On the Street

While out and about it's a good idea to be aware of your surroundings, especially in Montevideo. Thieves are common in the cities and will sometimes use violence to get what they want, so if you have the misfortune of being a victim of a robbery we recommend parting with your belongings straight away, as many thieves carry knifes or guns.

Grab-and-run robberies are a fairly regular occurrence in Montevideo. To avoid these make sure to pay particular attention to people on motorcycles, especially if there are two men together.

In face-to-face robberies, thieves steal mobile phones and even brand name shoes. With this in mind, it's not a good idea to walk with money, laptops or big cameras in view and unless you're in a crowded place, don't stop if someone asks you something, and don't take out your phone if they ask you the time. While on the street make sure to always have $10 - $20 ready in your pocket. That way you won't need to take out your whole wallet in case you meet someone looking for small change.

If you are in a crowd make sure to keep your bag hugged close to your chest, or clamped tightly under your arm. If you are going out at night, try to bring as little as possible with you and use your pockets instead of a bag.

In a Car

While traveling in a car with a bag, never leave it on top of the seat. This is because thieves have been known to break car windows to take bags, even at traffic lights. Instead keep it under your seat, between your legs.

Similarly, when you're not in the car, never leave anything visible through the car window, as it can attract thieves. Always leave your possessions under the seat or in the trunk/boot, or alternatively, take them with you.

Streets to be careful on

In Montevideo, the avenues where you're most likely to get robbed are: General Flores, José Belloni, Camino Maldonado, 8 de Octubre, José Batlle y Ordóñez (known as Propios), San Martín, Camino Carrasco and Avenida Italia. Other main junctions that are best avoided are: Mallorca and Pirán, Iguá and Mataojo, Iguá and Hipólito Irigoyen, Camino Carrasco and Oncativo, and Camino Carrasco and Juan Agazzi. Pay special attention when you are around these streets!

FEELING ABROAD TIPS

- **P**hotocopy all of your important documents before you leave and email them to yourself.

- Make sure your passport will be valid for the duration of the time you plan to be away.

- Cancel all of your subscriptions, wrap up your bills and inform your bank you are moving country.

- Fill all of your prescriptions before you go. Finding your medication might not be so easy.

- Don't forget to unblock your mobile phone before you leave.

- Clothes and shoes in Uruguay tend to be expensive, so make sure you have all you need before you move.

- Don't forget to pack things that are normal for you but will probably be hard to find in Uruguay. These will help minimise homesickness.

- Check the weather for all of the countries you will stop off in on the way. The last thing you want is to be too hot or too cold for your stop offs.

- Plan how you are going to get from the airport to your accommodation. You can use the links below to help.

  goo.gl/Dddeh7   **www.taxisaeropuerto.com** EN/PT

Don't forget to pick up a map at the airport.

Inflation in Uruguay can rise sharply, so don't be surprised if prices vary from month to month.

Discover Moving to Hong Kong

Moving to Hong Kong is full o first-hand information on wha it's really like to move to thi bustling metropolis. It is burstine with need-to-know information from big things like how to get a visa to smaller things, such a hidden costs that might take yo by surprise.

The guide is laid out in an easy to-read manner to avoi overwhelming the reader. We als provide links to useful website and apps that Hong Kon residents themselves use to mak their lives easier.

Inside Moving to Hong Kong:

- Language and culture help to put you in the Hong Kor mindset.

- A guide to expat renting and a breakdown of the differe neighbourhoods.

- An introduction to the school system with details of differe schools and crèches.

- Advice and references to help you decide if it is actual feasible to move.

- Personal tips coming straight from our experience a mistakes.

- Photos to show you day-to-day life in Hong Kong.

- A list of contacts for over 100 different hobbies to kick your social life.

- Over 30 categories full of relevant, up-to-date information

Photo Credits

Front Cover
Virginia Chappe

About Us
Claire & Juan

The Basics
Murga - Pablo Andrés
Cardozo Hernández

Choosing a Flight
Aeroplane - Amaszonas

International Shipping
Port - CucombreLibre
Containers - Maria TC

Restricted Items
Airport Security - María
Elena Bautista

Converting your Currency
Money - Anderson
Nascimento

Seasons and Time
Beach - Ivana Pilatos
Autumn Beatle -
Montecruz Foto
Stormy Sea - Vince Alongi
Rose Garden - Vince
Alongi

Suitable Translators
Dictionary - Andrés
Atehortua

Taxes
Paperwork - Andrés Nieto
Porras
Apartments - Jorge Gobbi
School - G.U.R.I.Inc

Banks
BANRED ATM - AEBU

Housing
Big House - Jimmy
Baikovicius
Aerial View - Jimmy
Baikovicius
Hotel Colón -
Casaseneleste
Sofitel - Jimmy
Baikovicius
Attached Houses - Lisa
Myr
Estate Agent - Beatrice
Church

Pink House - Vince Alongi
Boardwalk View - Jimmy
Baikovicius

Connecting Utilities
Light Bulb - Josep Ma.
Rosell
Tap - Jase Curtis
Router - Sarchi
Television - Iain Watson
Phone - Tom Page

Everyday Shops
Supermarket - Agustina
Pagliari
Greengrocer - Vince
Alongi
Abitab - Agustina
Pagliari
Redpagos - Agustina
Pagliari
Carpenter - Brian
Fitzharris
Food Market - Lionel
Ferrer

Local Entertainment
Beach - Ivana Pilatos
Food Stand - Jorge Gobbi
Barbeque - John Walker
Candombe Drummers -
Jimmy Baikovicius
Stadium - Jimmy
Baikovicius
Ballet - Jimmy
Baikovicius
Tour Bus - Andrés
Eduardo Perrone
Cabo Polonio -
Casaseneleste
Colonia - Philip Choi

Social and Hobbies
American Football - Vince
Alongi
Bocce - La Prensa
Drumming Group - Rod
Waddington
Tango - Maria TC
Street Football - John Seb
Barber
Golf - Jorge Gobbi
Paragliding - Nico Pereira
Boat - Vince Alongi
Paddling - Jimmy
Baikovicius

Getting Around
Tres Cruces - R Melgar
Taxi - Jimmy Baikovicius

Train – Marcelo Campi
Ferries - Liam Quinn
Bikes - Ivana Pilatos
Traffic Jam - Jimmy
Baikovicius

Disability Services
Braille - Stefan Malmesjö
Sign Language - Daveynin

Unexpected Costs
Bottle Bank - Agustina
Pagliari

Helpful Mobile Apps
Screen Shots - Juan I.
Pita

News
Screen Shots - Juan I.
Pita

Customs to get used to
Barbeque - Pacecharging
Merienda - Marcelenur
Football Supporters -
Jimmy Baikovicius

Religion
Catholic Church - John
Walker
Synagogue - Sefaradí
Iemanja - Jimmy
Baikovicius

Family Services
School Children -
Bicentenario Uruguay
Laptops - One Laptop per
Child
Children - Vince Alongi

Pets
Lupe - Hernán Pita
Cat - LWYang
Ziggy - Mariana
Nerguizian

Health
Pharmacy - Agustina
Pagliari

Staying Safe
Policemen - Mateo
Teperino

Back Cover
Marcelo Campi

Printed in Great Britain
by Amazon